Conten

Introduction

How about a pub lunch? There are 100 country pubs to choose from in this new guide, and there is something special about every one of them. There are pubs with so wide a choice of drinks that you won't know where to to start, there are others with mouth-watering menus, others so cosy that you won't want to leave, and some with play areas so exciting that your children won't want to leave! All you need to do is get there, and what better way to work up an appetite than to walk? There are gentle walks, strenuous climbs, walks with spectacular panoramic views, and others with interesting places to explore on the way. Most of the walks are circular routes, and all of them have a welcoming pub as the halfway point – so you can eat a hearty meal happy in the knowledge that by the time you return to your car, you will have walked it off!

The Pubs

The pubs have been chosen for a number of reasons, including the choice of real ales, lagers and ciders on draught, the high quality of the food available, and, of course, the genial atmosphere. We have aimed to give an idea of what the pub is like; its décor and ambience, the beverages on draught, the typical meals available together with the average prices, and the times food is served. We have indicated the establishments which impose restrictions as to the entry of children, dogs and muddy boots – while most pubs allow children in over a certain age, they are usually required to remain in a designated area, and dogs and dripping walking gear are sometimes relegated to the porch. Many pubs are renowned for their meals, so if you are planning to visit one of these places, it is usually a good idea to book in advance – we have suggested this in many establishments, and have provided telephone numbers. It is often a good idea to phone anyway, as arrangements change, and pubs themselves often have a change of management or tenancy, both of which can affect the whole style of the pub.

The Walks

At the beginning of each outing, we give an indication of the type of walk you should expect, whether it is a gentle walk through farmland, along the coast, or a strenuous climb through woods and up hills.

Whatever the walk, do wear sensible clothes and sturdy shoes – you can stumble even when the ground is level, and new clothes are likely to be spoilt if snagged by twigs and brambles. It is often a good idea to wear something waterproof as you never know when the heavens might open! Wellington

AA

SHORT WALKS

~ TO ~

COUNTRY PUBS

Scenic Walks ~ Good Food ~ Real Ale

Produced by the Publishing Division of the
Automobile Association.

Cover Design by Directions Limited.

Illustrations by Alan Roe and Pamela Hankey.

Printed and bound by Grosvenor Press
(Portsmouth) Ltd.

A CIP catalogue record for this book is available from
the British Library.

Published by The Automobile Association, Fanum
House, Basingstoke, Hampshire RG21 2EA.

ISBN 0 7495 0195 2

boots are recommended if it has been raining recently, or if you are likely to be using bridleways or walking through water meadows.

Don't carry anything with you, if you can help it, other than something you can tuck into a pocket. A bag of useful items might not seem very heavy when you set out, but you will soon be begging others to take it for a while. However, in hot weather, it is a good idea to put a small screw-top bottle of juice or water in your pocket, especially if there are children with you.

We have tried to find official parking area in which you can leave your car, but sometimes it has been necessary to use village high streets or farm lanes. Please take care not to obstruct local traffic, and remember that you will be gone for several hours.

We have not provided maps, but we have included Ordnance Survey map references, so while it is possible to undertake the walk purely by following the detailed route instructions, it is always a good idea to take a map with you.

Be aware that bridleways, slopes and farm tracks can become very slippery when wet so, where possible, walk on grass verges after a rainfall, as these will give you a better grip.

We have avoided using roads as much as possible, but sometimes it has been

necessary to include a stretch of road to achieve a circular route. On roads, keep children and dogs close to you at all times, for peaceful country lanes can be deceptive, you never know what's around the next corner. Please also ensure that all walkers keep to the right-hand side of the road, facing oncoming traffic.

Keep dogs on a lead when approaching other walkers and farm animals – your pet may have a friendly disposition, but it doesn't always seem that way when you are on the receiving end.

Farm animals, especially huge cows, can be quite an obstacle when they are crowding around a stile. Don't despair, all you need to do to move them is to walk on, quietly saying 'hup, hup', and they will soon be out of your way.

Stiles are there for walkers, so use them, and where you have to pass through gates, make sure you close them behind you.

Paths are not always signposted and are sometimes difficult to see, which is why we have provided such detailed directions. On a single walk, you may find that one landowner has made the effort to provide clear signs and well-constructed stiles, while his neighbour has allowed paths to become overgrown, ploughed up, and even obstructed by fencing or barbed wire! Don't let this put you off, for public footpaths are a right of way and for you to enjoy.

Weston *to* Branscombe

Approximately 6 miles

Coastal walk along part of the East Devon footpath affording fine views of Beer Head, Portland Bill and Torbay. The scrub-covered hillside accommodates badgers, and the undisturbed undergrowth of the coast slips is perfect for finches and warblers. Buzzards and kestrels can also be seen.

Parking

OS Map Ref SY1688 Leave your car at the NT car park at Weston.

Further Exploration

Branscombe is a scattered village of pretty, stone, thatched cottages nestling in three deep combes. There you will find an old forge, built of wood and still working, and a bakery which still produces bread from ovens fired by faggots.

St. Winifred's Church was built in the 12th century, and there still remain fragments of a medieval wall-painting, probably representing Belshazzar's Feast.

*F*ollow the NT signs southwest to Weston Combe until you reach the coastal path, turn left and follow this path for nearly two miles – do not bear left onto the South Devon Coast Path after Weston Cliff. Soon after passing the fort remains on your left, you will come to a junction of footpaths. Take the right-hand path signposted to Branscombe Mouth. At the car park, turn left by the stream and follow the path across the meadows to Branscombe,where you turn left to the pub.

Mason's Arms (Free House)

This is a popular, creeper-clad, 14th-century inn with a pretty terrace and colourful gardens which have ample seating. Inside the low-beamed, rambling pub, there is a massive central hearth – spit roasts are cooked here during winter on Thursday lunchtimes – around which chairs, cushioned wall benches and settles, are arranged on the flagstones. Children are not allowed in the bar.

On draught: Bass, Hall & Woodhouse Badger Best and Tanglefoot, Guinness, Tennents Pilsner, Hofbrau. Food: There is a wide range at lunchtime, from ploughman's lunches at £2.50, to venison and mushroom pie at £3.80, to curry at £4.50. Food is served at 12-1.45pm, and is limited in the evening as there is a separate restaurant.
Telephone: (029780) 300.

*T*urn right out of the inn, towards Upper Branscombe and walk along the lane until you reach St. Winifred's Church. Take the footpath through the churchyard, which will bring you out in the woods above the combe. Turn right and climb up towards Berry Barton, making sure to keep right when the path forks. At Berry Barton, follow the quiet lane west for about a mile back to Weston.

Approximately 6½ miles   ## Start Point *to* East Prawle

*L*eave the car park through a gate and follow a path towards Great Mattiscombe Sand, down to the coast. Join the main coastal footpath and follow this to Lannacombe Beach. Remain on the coastal path back to Start Point and on towards Prawle Point – the extreme southern tip of Devon. The word 'Prawle' comes from an old English word meaning "look-out hill". The rocky path soon levels onto grassland near Maelcombe House. Towards the end of the grassland above the long shingle beach, follow a sign pointing to East Prawle, to a gate, up a steep grassy hill, and over a wall. Follow the road into the village.

Coastal walk passing a number of coves and beaches, with a contrasting return walk across undulating farmland with views inland of typical rolling Devon hills. Wildlife is abundant: look out for finches, pipits, cormorants, gulls and colourful aromatic flowers and shrubs.

Pig's Nose (Free House)

Located close to a small green at the centre of this hilltop village, this unpretentious white-walled pub follows an unusual theme inside, with pig posters and a cabinet of pig ornaments. Children are welcome.

On draught: Flower's IPA, Wadworth 6X, Murphy's Stout, Heineken, Fosters. Food: Menu offers honey-roast ham (£3.20), plaice and chips (£3.40) and ploughmans from £2.40. Of particular note are the sandwiches, including fresh crab (£2.10), prawn (£1.80) and cheese (£1.25). Food is served at 12-2pm and 6-10pm. Telephone: (054851) 209.

Parking

OS Map 202 Ref SX8237 Start Point car park (70p per day, supervised during the summer).

Further Exploration

A short diversion can be made to Start Point lighthouse where fine views can be had across to Slapton Sands and Dartmouth. The lighthouse directs those vessels sailing in-shore, to avoid the Skerries, a dangerous bank off the coast.

*F*rom the pub, continue along the road to a T-junction, turn right, and right again at a phone box. Follow the lane, ignoring the turning to Maelcombe House. Paths are waymarked with blue arrows on posts, through two farms – Woodcombe and Higher Borough – and across fields. Remain on path down a steep combe to a road, bear right and follow signposts back to Start Point.

Burrator Reservoir to Meavy

Approximately 5½ miles

This walk through moorland, woodland and open meadows offers panoramic views to Plymouth and the sea, across Bodmin Moor, of Dartmoor tors, and into Cornwall. Look out for Dartmoor ponies, deer, rabbits, and buzzards.

Parking

OS Maps 191 and 200 Ref SX5669 Far end of Burrator Reservoir.

Follow the lane to the south of the reservoir until you reach a track on the left leading to a gate. Pass through this, keeping left of the woodland, through another gate, and bear right, following an established grassy path through bracken, keeping the wall and enclosed woodland to your right. The path is marked by a pink dot on stones and trees. Remain on this path through two gates and follow the wall to join a track, and bear right downhill to a quiet lane. Turn left into the peaceful hamlet of Sheepstor, then right, opposite a stone cross. Over a bridge, take the footpath on the right signposted to Markhams Cross, marked with a yellow dot. This path crosses meadows through oak woodlands, and eventually past Yeo Farm to a peaceful lane. Bear right, cross a cattle grid and then some stepping stones across the river, into Meavy village and head towards the church.

From the pub, take the lane uphill away from the green, bear left at T-junction, then right into a lane signposted to Burrator, and take the grassy path on left onto Yennadon Down. Reaching a wide, established path (the course of an old railway), bear right and follow through coniferous woodland, with the reservoir down to the right. Cross a quiet lane and turn right into a second lane, down to the reservoir edge and parking area.

Royal Oak (Free House)

 This pretty whitewashed pub is set beside the church and the village green. There are a few picnic benches outside, and roses and hanging baskets add a splash of colour. It is named after the ancient oak tree on the green which is said to have been planted while the church was being built. There are two bars, one with red banquette seating, wall-benches, small wooden tables, beamed ceiling, open fires and numerous prints adorning the walls. The smaller, public bar has a large fireplace and a more rustic feel. Children are not allowed inside.

On draught: Furguson Dartmoor Strong, Courage Best, Guinness, Castlemaine 4X, Kronenbourg 1664. Food: There are generous portions of simple pub meals – various ploughmans (from £1.90), soup (90p), chilli and rice £2.50, apple pie and cream (£1.20). Food is served at 12-2pm and 6.30pm-9pm. Telephone: (0822) 852944

Becky Falls *to* Lustleigh   Approximately 5½ miles

Outstanding views across beautiful countryside and into wooded river valleys, are the essence of this walk along the edge of Dartmoor. The network of trails takes you through the Bovey Valley nature reserve, the home of flycatchers, warblers, dippers and wagtails and a splendid array of wild flowers.

Parking

OS Map 191 Ref SK7580. Becky Falls car park (Open 10am-6pm £1.50 per day).

 *F*ollow the road right signposted to Becky Falls, then turn left, cross the footbridge and take the path to Bovey Valley and Lustleigh Cleave. The falls soon become visible on the right, and signposted. Remain on the path through mixed forest with Becky Brook down to the right, over the junction and along the trail which gradually drops down into the heavily wooded Bovey Valley. Two-thirds of the way down, bear right at a wall, towards Clam Bridge. Cross the bridge and keep to the path gently climbing up the side of the valley. At a fork, follow a path waymarked Lustleigh via Pethybridge, to a track and then a road along which you bear right, then first left – Pethybridge. Fork right at a telephone box and walk down into the heart of the village. The pub is tucked down behind the church, close to the cricket ground.

The Cleave (Free House)

 This is a beautiful, white-painted, 15th-century thatched inn. Its old flagstone porch is surrounded by a neat and colourful garden which offers some very peaceful shelter in summer. Inside, a comfortable, welcoming lounge bar has a low, beamed ceiling, high-backed settles, wall seats and wheel-backed chairs. A second bar and further room are more plainly furnished and house the dartboard, pool table and fruit machines. Children are welcome in the family room.

 On draught: Marston Pedigree, Bass, Flower's IPA, Murphy's Stout, Heineken. Food: Basic menu includes home-made soup (£1.50), coq au vin (£5.25), and rack of lamb (£8.10). Desserts range from chocolate mousse to treacle tart (£1.60). Service is pleasant and efficient, and portions generous. Food is served at 12-2.30pm and 7-8.30pm. Telephone: (06477) 223.

 *L*eaving the pub, pass the church and follow the road signposted to Rudge, up a steep hill. At the T-junction, take the footpath ahead waymarked to Bovey Valley, into which the well-defined path descends after skirting Hisley Farm, gradually winding down to an ancient packhorse bridge over the river. Pass through a gate and bear right onto an established track, signposted to Manaton. Keep on this path back over the river and up the steep valley, rejoining your outward route, and return to Becky Falls.

Further Exploration
Becky Falls
Set in 60 acres of glorious natural woodlands, Becky Brook cascades through a fairy glen and crashes 70 feet over huge granite boulders.

Lustleigh is a charming village, containing numerous thatched cottages and a 13th-century church with an unusual rood-screen bearing the pomegranate badge of Catherine of Aragon.

Torcross *to* Slapton

Approximately 5 miles

This walk offers coastal views along Slapton Sands, and a peaceful nature trail alongside the Ley with its abundant wildlife and reedbeds.

Parking:
OS Map 202 Ref SX8242
Torcross Car Park.

Further Exploration

Torcross
Pleasant old houses line the seafront along Start Bay at Torcross. The village was once the most easterly fishing village to fish for pilchards until the pilchard shoals disappeared from the south-west coast.

Slapton
Many houses in its twisting streets have had their walls rendered to hide shell damage. During the war, the US army took over the village for manoeuvres. It is dominated by a great tower, north of the church, which is 80ft high and built of slate and is the remains of a College of Chantry Priests founded in 1373. The church has a 14th-century medieval spire.

*F*rom Torcross car park either follow the path beside Slapton Ley eastwards, between the road and Ley, or cross the road and walk along the top of the beach. Follow the ridge or Ley path to a memorial and take the road signposted to Slapton on the left. Cross the bridge over the stream and reedbeds at the end of the Ley and enter the nature reserve through a gate on the left. Follow the nature trail through reeds and woodland to the north of the Ley until you reach a path off to your left, signposted 'Slapton via Broad Walk'. This path, created on boards above the marshy grounds, weaves for short distance across the reedbeds, giving you an excellent chance to see warblers, gulls, duck and the odd buzzard soaring across neighbouring fields. Keep to the path signposted 'Deer Bridge' until you reach a quiet lane, then turn right and follow the road uphill then down into the attractive village of Slapton, which lies sheltered in a hollow of the South Hams hills.

*R*eturn to the lane, bear left and follow it through the village, turning left past the Post Office and keeping to the lane back down to Slapton Ley and the beach. Turn right towards the car.

Tower Inn (Free House)

This is a neat white-washed building next
to the remains of the large tower. An
ancient 14th-century inn, this was once a
row of cottages for the workers who helped to build
the monastory of which only the tower remains.
Inside, the air of antiquity is preserved in the three
bars, with flagstone floors, low-backed settles, and
small armchairs. One bar has a wood-burning stove
and one has a log fire within a bare stone wall. Tables
in the landscaped garden make a relaxing spot for an
evening drink, the ivy-covered tower dominating the
scene. Children are welcome in the restaurant, side
room and garden.

On draught: The Tower is renowned for its excellent
range of ales, usually ten on handpump, including
Hall & Woodhouse Badger Best and Tanglefoot,
Eldridge Pope Royal Oak, Gibbs Mew Bishop's
Tipple, Palmer IPA, Ruddles County, Wadworth 6X,
Guinness, Stella Artois. Food: Good range of food,
especially Italian dishes, includes various pastas (from
£3.25) and large 8" pizza's with numerous toppings
(around £6.20) and steaks, basket meals, ploughmans
and sandwiches. Food is served at 12-2.30pm and
7-9.30pm. Telephone: (0548) 580216

Chagford *to* Drewesteignton

Approximately 7½ miles

A peaceful walk along the River Teign exploring the wooded river bank, rich in flora and fauna, and a panoramic high-level track offering views towards the high tors of Dartmoor and into the Teign Gorge.

Parking
OS Map 191 Ref SK7087
Chagford car park.

Further Exploration
Chagford is a traditional moorland town and was one of the three stannary towns to which tinners brought their metal for assay and stamping.

Drewsteignton is a compact village with mainly thatched, granite cottages and a late 15th-century church at the far end of its square.

Castle Drogo (National Trust)
This imposing granite castle stands on a rocky crag 900ft above the River Teign. It is a combination of medieval might and 20th-century luxury, best appreciated for the interior, but there are wonderful views from the gardens.
Telephone: (0647) 33306

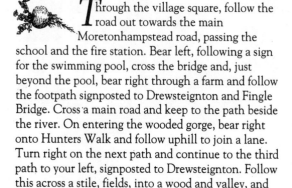

Through the village square, follow the road out towards the main Moretonhampstead road, passing the school and the fire station. Bear left, following a sign for the swimming pool, cross the bridge and, just beyond the pool, bear right through a farm and follow the footpath signposted to Drewsteignton and Fingle Bridge. Cross a main road and keep to the path beside the river. On entering the wooded gorge, bear right onto Hunters Walk and follow uphill to join a lane. Turn right on the next path and continue to the third path to your left, signposted to Drewsteignton. Follow this across a stile, fields, into a wood and valley, and up to a road where you turn left into the village.

Drewe Arms (Whitbread)

This rustic village pub has changed little since before the war. It is a low, thatched, cream-coloured building in the peaceful village square, next to the church – a popular venue for Morris Men in the summer. Inside, ochre walls are decorated with local team photographs. There is no serving counter – the ale is kept on racks in a tap-room at the back and you order through a hatchway.

On draught: Flower's Original, Wadworth 6X
Food: Ham or cheese and chutney sandwiches (£1) are available at 12-2pm. Telephone: (0647) 21224.

Leave the square and follow the road down towards Fingle Bridge. Near the bottom of the hill, take the footpath over a stile on your left down into the valley and onto a road, bearing left towards Fingle Bridge. Before you reach the bridge, pass through a gate on the left and follow a path beside the river until you join the outward route at the edge of the gorge and return to Chagford.

Fowey *to* Polkerris

Approximately 6½ miles.

 *F*ollow footpath signs to the town centre. At the general store, bear right and follow the road down into Readymoney Cove, and then join the coastal footpath up into Carington Wood. At the first bend, bear right and follow Love Lane, heading inland. At a quiet lane, turn left and then right at a T-junction towards a small hamlet. At Lankelly Farm, take the footpath on the left down into a combe and follow the yellow stickers across stiles, through meadows, and past two farms . At a lane beside Tregaminion church, turn right and then left through the first gate. You will soon join the coast path down through a wood to the small fishing hamlet of Polkerris.

Rashleigh Inn (Free House)

 This marvellously placed pub has picnic tables on its stone terrace overlooking an isolated beach and small jetty. Inside local photographs and prints adorn the panelled walls. There is a small restaurant area where children are welcome.

On draught: St Austell Hicks Special and Bosuns, Furguson Dartmoor Strong, Tetley Bitter, Guinness, Stella Artois. Food: Menu includes stock pot soup (£1), sandwiches from £1.20, fish pie (£4.50), cottage pie (£4), and an interesting salad bar. Food is served at 12-2pm and 7-10.30pm (Sunday 7-9.45pm). Sandwiches are served all day in summer. Telephone: (072681) 3991.

*L*eaving the pub, retrace your steps back through the woods, remaining on the coastal footpath. This path is a fine undulating cliff walk, crossing National Trust land, namely Gribbin Head and its 84ft beacon built in 1832 to help vessels navigate safely around the headland. From Gribbin head, the established path undulates down into small isolated caves and valleys. The path eventually rejoins the outward route at Love Lane to central Fowey.

The outward route takes you along flower-filled paths, woodland and open meadow; the contrasting return route is a coastal walk over cliffs and down into coves with fine views across the estuary, of Polman and of the china clay area near St Austell.

Parking

OS Map 200 Ref SX1251 Main Fowey car park (£1 per day).

Further Exploration

Fowey is one of Cornwall's most historic and romantic places, with its narrow lanes and colourful old houses. Large tankers anchor in the deep waters of the estuary as they are loaded with china clay – Fowey remains one of Cornwall's leading exporters. An exhibition describing the town's history can be found in the Town Hall Museum.

St Catherine's Castle (English Heritage) was one of the many strongholds built by Henry VIII to defend the coast. It was restored in 1855 and is open daily (free).

Polkerris was one of the busiest fishing harbours of the last century. Beside the beach are the ruins of the old 'pilchard palace', one of the largest in Cornwall. Here the pilchards were 'baulked' in salted piles and pressed for their oil.

Gurnard's Head *to* Zennor   Approximately 4 miles

A beautiful coastal walk taking in some of the North Cornwall Coast Path, with magnificent sea views, combining a steep climb over rugged terrain, and a gentle return journey across wide pastures.

Parking

OS Map 203 Ref SU3744 Gurnard's Head Hotel car park off the B3306.

Further Exploration

Zennor Church was built in the 12th century church probably on the site of an ancient chapel. It is famous for the mermaid chair in the side chapel, and the romantic legend that goes with it.

Wayside Museum, Zennor
This quaint private museum was founded in 1935 by Col 'Freddie' Hirst and is now owned by curators Richard and Betty Williamson. The main theme of the museum is life in Zennor from 3000BC to the 1930's. Telephone (0736) 79645

*T*urn left from the car park and take the Treen Farm drive way first left past the hotel. This leads past the farm and becomes a dirt track winding down to the Coast Guard lookout on Gurnard's Head. Continue past a ruin below which the North Cornwall coast path crosses this track and is clearly signposted. Turn right at this point and follow the well-defined path to Zennor. After a series of steps up to a junction marked by a National Trust plaque for Zennor Head, turn right over a stile and continue to Zennor.

*T*urn right out of the pub, pass the Wayside Museum, and turn right into first farm gate, which has a dirt track leading past the farm buildings to a field ahead. The start of the footpath is not clearly marked – if in doubt, ask the local farmers, they are very friendly. A stile affords access to this field. Once over, cross the field to a gap in the far wall marked by a white post, and follow this route through subsequent fields. Keep the main B3306 road to your left; the footpath eventually joins this as you pass several houses on your right. Follow the road for a short distance until the Gurnard's Head Hotel comes into view on the horizon. Look for a gap by a black farm gate on your right where the telegraph poles leave the road, and cross the fields towards the hotel. There are three fields to cross to complete your walk. Cross the first field with the wall on your left, but once through the stile to the second field, keep the wall to your right, and you will finish in front of the hotel.

Tinners Arms (Free House)

This 12th century, stone and granite building is a friendly, traditional country pub consisting of a narrow room with bench seating, a single bar, and open hearth fires at both ends of the room. There is ample sheltered seating at the front of the pub, and a large patio to the side. Lunch time is very busy during the summer. Children are permitted in the children's room and the restaurant.

On draught: St Austell Tinners Ale and Hicks Special, Carlsberg, Guinness, and a selection of local keg beers. Food: Basic menu offers ploughman's lunches (£2.50), salads (£2.95), soup (£1.50), lasagne and pies (£2.95 - £3.20). Food is served at 12-2pm and 6-10pm. A wider choice of afternoon teas and evening meals is available in the new restaurant. Telephone: (0736) 796927

Coombe *to* Morwenstow   Approximately 6½ miles

This walk takes you along remote, wild cliffs, with magnificent views of the dramatic coastline, through deep, green valleys, rolling farmland and tranquil wooded river trails. On such a quiet stretch of coast, wildlife is abundant – watch out for buzzards, raven, jackdaws, rock pipits and a few species of gull.

Parking

OS Map 190 Ref SS2011 National Trust car park (donations).

Further Exploration

Morwenstow is Cornwall's northernmost parish, and is best known for its former vicar – the poet, Robert Stephen Hawker, who came to this small parish in 1834 and spent 40 years serving a multitude of smugglers, wreckers and dissenters. An extraordinary man, he was concerned for the fate of mariners wrecked on this coast and often scrambled down the high cliffs to carry the bodies up to the church for a Christian burial – each has their own grave, but no headstone.

*F*rom the car, follow the coastal path (waymarked) on your right, which wends its way round a few headlands down into steep, unspoilt combes. Don't be put off by the white dish aerials, these are soon left behind. At the second combe – Tidna Combe – follow the footpath inland, soon running beside a small stream. The path passes through varied vegetation which changes as one leaves the harsher conditions of the coast. The taller plants and shrubs begin to dominate and the valley becomes very sheltered and alive with insect and birdlife. Follow the path to the end of the valley, up some steps to the stile, across a field uphill to another stile, before entering the far corner of the pub's garden in the village of Morwenstow.

The Bush (Free House)

This delightful ancient country pub is very welcoming, reputed to be one of the very oldest in Britain. It was once a monastic rest-house on a pilgrim route, and parts date back to 950 when it was a hermit's cell. Of particular note is the Celtic piscinia carved from serpentine stone still set in one wall. The three bars have heavily slate flagged floors, the main bar being quite small with ancient built-in settles, and a huge stone fireplace, while the snug side has antique seats, old elm trestle tables and walls decorated with miner's lamps, casks, funnels, blue plates, clocks and various prints of the pub. The small windows offer views across the fields and out to sea. No children under 14 are allowed in the bars but there is some seating out in sunken courtyard.

On draught: St Austell Hicks Special and Tinners Ale, Worthington Best, Bass, Inch's Cider. Food: The short lunchtime menu offers good value for money – soup (£1), beef stew and roll (£1.75), ploughmans (£1.75), pasty (£1.10) and sandwiches (£1). Food is served at 12-2pm. Closed Mondays in October - March. Telephone: (028883) 242.

*R*etrace your route back down into Tidna Combe as far as the river. Cross over the bridge and the stile, and follow the edge of the field to another stile and on to a track. To the left is Toracombe, a 15th-century Tudor manor house. Pass through a gate on to arable fields. When the crop is high, walk along the edge of two fields, crossing the stiles before reaching a lane and Stanbury Farm. Walk up the driveway to the farm, keeping the house to your right and the pond to your left, to a gate. Follow the waymarked yellow arrows across two fields to join a lane at Eastaway Manor. Cross the lane and pass through a gate, keeping to the path beside the Manor. Cross a stile and continue following the arrows across the fields to the hamlet of Woodford, emerging on a lane opposite the chapel. Bear right, then right again at a thatched cottage, and follow the lane past a farm before joining the waymarked path to the right. Remain on this across the fields and through a gate down into the valley, making sure when entering woodland to take the track which runs at right angles to that which you are following, down to a small stream. Follow the yellow arrows on posts across the stream, then bear right and follow the beautiful wooded valley down towards Coombe valley. At the road, bear right down into the hamlet of Coombe. Keep on the quiet lane and follow the sign to Duckpool back to the beach.

The church of St Morwenna is superbly situated, almost in a dell between the cliffs towering to a height of 450ft on either side. In the valley, a small stream flows towards the sea. Its tower has always been a landmark for passing ships. The doorway is carved with heads of men and beasts, and inside are some fine Norman arches and well-carved bench ends.

Robert Hawker's eccentricity is shown in the rectory next to the church, with its unusual chimneys – modelled on the towers of churches he had known, and one on his mother's tomb. A few hundred yards south along the coastpath is 'Hawker's Hut', built of driftwood, where the parson wrote much of his poetry.

St Anthony-in-Meneage to Helford

Approximately 4¼ miles

A beautiful wooded shoreline and estuary walk through a very tranquil landscape . Birds likely to be seen on the walk include cormorants, many herons, shelduck, curlews and kingfishers.

Parking

OS Map 204 SW7825
St Antony-in-Meneage car park, close to parish church.

Further Exploration

The area incorporating Helford, Manaccan and St Anthony, forms the Lizard Peninsula known as Mereage – 'Monkish land'. Celtic monks brought christianity to the district, and formed hermitages and settlements, out of which arose the earliest churches of Cornwall.

St Antony-in-Meneage has a beautiful church, which stands only 30 yards from the edge of Gillan Creek. The remote and romantic position of the church may have given rise to the traditional story that the church was built by a band of shipwrecked Normans – built in St Anthony's honour for saving their lives. Some credibility is given to this tale by the fact that the town is built of a granite found only in Normandy. The church is lit by candlelight - brass candle holders hang from

*L*eave the car park, turning left onto a quiet lane passing the church and a small boat park on the edge of the creek. Keep to the lane until the second corner, where you pass through a gate on the right to join the coastal footpath. Keep to the coastal path through the heavily wooded slopes of the Helford river, down into small coves and beaches. It is important to keep only to the footpath through the wooded areas from St Antony because the land is owned by the Basaham estate. No dogs are allowed on this stretch. When the footpath meets a quiet lane, bear right and then left onto the coast path just past a house called the 'Old Pichard Shed'. Follow this path to Helford. Cross the footbridge over the creek and follow the lane to the pub.

*R*eturn across the footbridge, bear right and follow the footpath, signposted to Manaccan, to a heavily wooded valley with a small stream and active birdlife. The path gradually winds up out of the woods and crosses a meadow, road and a second field into the small village of Manaccan. Reaching a second road, cross by the antique shop and follow the lane down to the church. From there, follow the bridleway (waymarked) opposite the church gate and remain on this until you reach a lane at the creek side. Turn left and follow the lane along Gillan Creek back to the car park.

Shipwright's Arms (Cornish Brewery)

This fine thatched pub has a terrace dropping down to the water's edge, offering a peaceful, secluded view of this lovely wooded creek. Picnic benches sit amongst palm trees and flowers, and the pub entrance is decorated by colourful hanging baskets. Inside, there are comfortable oak settles and an open fire. A nautical theme is created by collections of model ships, sea pictures, navigational lamps, and drawings of people in the pub or village in years past. Children are welcome in the eating area or on the terrace.

On draught: John Devenish Dry Hop Bitter and Cornish Original, Newquay Traditional Steam Bitter, Guinness, Heineken. Food: There is a wide range of meat, fish, cheese, and pasties, and a good salad bar. Ploughmans and salads are all around £4. Hot dishes or summer barbeque in evenings. Food is served at 12-1.30pm and 7pm-9pm. No bar food on Sunday evenings in winter. Telephone: (032623) 235.

the town is built of a granite found only in Normandy. The church is lit by candlelight – brass candle holders hang from the ceiling – and a candlelit evensong is held.

A short diversion can be made along the coastal path to 'Dennis Head' (corruption of Cornish word Dinas, meaning castle), once an Iron-age cliff castle.

Helford is a snug village with small, white-washed thatched cottages tucked away by the creek, and other houses perched up on the hillside. Helford once had reputation as a smugglers haunt, and there are still cellars which are reputed to have been their secret stores.

Frenchman's Creek, made famous by Daphne du Maurier's novel of that name, lies a short distance to the west of Helford.

Manaccan, believed to date from 967, is a small village of cottages clustering around its ancient church which has a fig tree growing out of the south-west wall. This has taken root in the rubble between two outer stones and is known to have been growing for two hundred years.

Porthgwarra *to* Treen

Approximately 4½ miles

This is a rugged coastline walk, with dramatic headlands contrasting with sheltered sandy beaches, followed by a quiet farmland return route.

Parking

OS Map 203 Ref SW3621
Porthgwarra car park. (50p)

Further Exploration

The Minack Theatre is an incredible Greek-style amphitheatre founded by Miss Ravena Cade in 1931. It is hewn out of the cliffside 70 metres above the sea and offers audiences a spectacular natural backdrop. Productions are staged during the summer months in the evenings, and the theatre is open to viewing at a charge during the day.

Porthcurno beach is a broad stretch of white sand in a cove sheltered by jagged arms of granite. Much of the beach is made up of minute white shells and it was here that the first transatlantic cable was brought ashore. Take care on the steep path down to it.

Logan Rock weighs over 65 tons, and can be rocked. In 1824, 12 sailors dislodged it, but the Admiralty insisted that they replace it.

*B*ear left past the small shop, keeping the beach to your right. Follow the waymarked coastal path uphill past a house before heading right along the cliff top. Remain on the coastal path to the isolated and spectacular cove of Porth Chapel with its sandy beach. The path passes St Levern Holy Well (whose water is still used for baptisms) and ancient stone steps lead down to the beach and the site of a ruined chapel. Follow the footpath up onto the headland of Pean-Men-An-Mere (where there are remains of a radio mast – Cable and Wireless Company's attempt to monitor Marconi's experiment) and onto Pothcurno, where the path passes the Minack Theatre. Keep to the coastal path until you reach a National Trust sign, then take the path on the left inland over the fields to the village of Treen.

Logan Rock (St Austell)

Owned by the National Trust, this old and unspoilt inn has great charm and character with a low-beamed, rambling bar containing high-backed modern oak settles, wall seats and tables, and a large fireplace. There is also a snug, and a family bar at the rear where food can be ordered. A small attractive garden with tables looks out over open fields and there are also picnic tables in the front courtyard. Children are welcome in the garden and the family room, and dogs are allowed in on a lead. Make a point of looking at the different pictures on either side of the inn sign.

On draught: Tinners Ale, Hicks Special, Bosuns, Guinness, Carlsberg. Food: A good choice of basic bar food is served in generous portions. The menu ranges from lentil soup (£1.40), sandwiches (from £1.25), lasagne and salad (£3.25), baked potatoes and fillings from (£1.25) and ploughmans (£2.30). Food is served at 12-1.30pm and 7-9pm. Baby foods can be heated on request. Telephone: (073672) 495.

*R*eturn back up the lane past the tea rooms and, at the corner, bear left, heading towards the thatched cottage. Take the track between the houses immediately on your left towards a gate, and then follow the path across five fields and into Trendrennan Farm. Go through the farmyard, following the footpath sign, and head towards three masts ahead, crossing three fields and gates. Pass close to the post holding mast wire, cross a stile and bear right down the slope onto a track and along to the lane. Cross the road onto another track, through a gate, and across a field to Rospeath Farm. Through the gate, follow the clear path across two fields towards St Leven's Church, and enter the churchyard over the stile. Reaching the road, bear left and, in a short distance, take the footpath on your right and bear right again at a junction, following the path which soon rejoins the outward route back along the coastal path to Porthgwarra.

Kennisham Hill *to* Luxborough

Approximately 5 miles

Quiet walk through the woods and valleys of the Brendon hills, with panoramic views across neighbouring hills towards Watchet and across to the Welsh coast. Plenty of pheasants and buzzards can be seen in this area.

Parking

OS Map 181 Ref SS9635 Picnic area beside B3224

Further Exploration

Combe Sydenham Country Park, Monksilver
A few miles east of Luxborough is a 16th-century house that was once the home of Sir Francis Drake's second wife, Elizabeth. There is an Elizabethan-style garden with woodland walks, a corn mill and a children's play area. Fly fishing is also available. Telephone: (0984) 56284.

From the picnic area, follow the path on the left, waymarked to Wheddon Cross and Luxborough. Walk through coniferous woodland until, approaching a farm, you follow the path through a gateway and bear right, keeping to the edge of the woodland, continuing through fields and gates. At a junction of paths, head downhill towards Luxborough, keeping to the hedge when you enter the field, until you pass through a gate and bear right onto a track towards the river and a farm. Before you reach the stream, turn right through a gateway and cross two fields parallel to river to reach quiet lane and a small bridge. Turn right, uphill, then take footpath arrowed off to your left. Pass behind an old caravan onto an established path beside a small stream through mixed woodland. Cross a small footpath, bear right to a stile, and follow the path to a lane and the pub.

Turn left out of the pub, then right at a telephone box, and follow the quiet lane out of the village. Cross a small bridge and turn right, following a path uphill, soon turning left onto a track waymarked to Wheddon Cross via Colly Hill. Pass a pond and a cottage, turn right then, at a signpost, bear right to follow a path and pass through a gateway. On nearing a house tucked down in the valley, bear right, following red painted markers on posts, through a gate and along the edge of a wood. After passing through a further gate into the coniferous forest, follow the red markers up through woodland, bearing right on the main track, up past a game reserve for breeding pheasant. Follow the red markers through a gate and across a field, crossing a brook before going uphill through mixed woodland. Pass through another gate and cross a field downhill, before passing through a gate onto a forest track. In a short distance, take the waymarked path uphill through a clearing, bearing left at the top, and follow the forest track back to the picnic area.

Royal Oak (Free House)

This is a pub of great charm and antiquity within Exmoor National Park, located deep down within a valley in the Brendon Hills. Known locally as the 'Blazing Stump', it dates back to the 15th-century and remains totally unspoilt, with flagstone and cobbled floors, inglenook fireplaces, and beamed ceilings. There are three bars with a mixture of seating from rustic benches to armchairs. The real bar of character has a massive open fire and the welcome is warm and friendly. There is a charming garden plus a bench out in the front near the quiet lane. Children are welcome.

On draught: Eldridge Pope Royal Oak, Flower's IPA, Golden Hill Exmoor Ale, Cotleigh Tawny Ale, Carlsberg, Guinness. Food: Good value bar snacks include soup (£1.50), beef and Beamish pie (£4.95), lamb curry (£3.45), vegetable and stilton pie (£3.45), and ploughmans (from £2.95). Puddings include apple pie and blackberry and apple pie (both £1.35, with custard £1.65). Food is served at 12-2pm (not Sunday) and 7-10pm (Sunday 7-9.30pm). Telephone: (0984) 40319.

Bridgetown *to* Winsford   Approximately 5½ miles

*This walk is quite
strenuous in places as
there are some steep
hills, but the
magnificent views of
the Exe Valley make it
well worth the effort.*

Parking
OS Map 181 Ref SS9233.
Lay-by on A396.

Further Exploration
Winsford
Winsford, set on the edge of
Exmoor National Park, is ideally
situated for walking, riding,
shooting and fishing. Within 1¾
miles is the Caratacus Stone on
Winsford Hill thought to have
been inscribed in the Dark Ages.
On the same hill are the
Wambarrows – three buried
mounds probably of the Beaker
period of Bronze age and
between 2,500 and 4,000 year
old.

Walk into the village along the main road, past the post office, and take the road on the left signposted 'Caravan Site'. Cross over the River Exe and take the footpath on the right signposted to Coppleham, and follow the river through the meadows. Continue to a small gate and bridleway sign on the left away from the river and follow the path to join a lane. Bear right, cross the river, then turn left onto a footpath waymarked 'Paths to Howetown'. At the first house, pass through a gate in front of the house to another gate, then follow the path uphill before dropping down slightly to continue along the edge of a small wood. Once through another gate, walk beside the river and keep to the valley path until you reach another gate (signposted). Follow this path uphill through woodland then, near a gate, fork right uphill, soon crossing the edge of a field to yet another gate and a track. Bear left down the track to a metalled road and the hamlet of Howetown. Keep to this very quite lane over a bridge into Winsford. Cross the main road and bear left for the pub.

Royal Oak (Free House)

 This is a fine 14th-century thatched inn in picturesque Winsford, a quaint village of thatched cottages. Inside, the lounge bar is partly panelled, with good bay window seats overlooking the village green and the River Winn. Even the bar is panelled and close to it is the huge inglenook fireplace with a fine iron fireback. Comfortable seating is provided by Windsor chairs and stools around sturdy wooden tables. Children are welcome in the eating area.

On draught: Flower's IPA and Original, Guinness, Heineken, Stella Artois. Food: Good bar food from a regularly changing menu includes soup (£1.35), fish paté (£3.90), ploughmans (from £3.70), sandwiches (from £1.45), and fish crumble (£5.70). Food is served at 12-2pm (1.30pm on Sunday) and 7.30-9.30pm. Telephone: (064385) 232 and 455.

*T*urn left out of the pub, follow the lane uphill past a hotel on the right and take the track on the left waymarked to Dulverton, Tarr Stopps and Winsford Hill. Follow this old route uphill over the moorland and down into a beautiful combe. At a small brook, cross a footbridge and bear left, following the yellow signs. Joining the main path, bear left and walk downhill to a gate, then turn right and follow the path uphill. At a fork, bear left and then, at further junctions, keep right on the main path up to a gate. Cross the field and, after two gates, bear right, then left onto a quiet metalled lane and follow this back down into Bridgetown, joining the main road back to the car.

Kingston *to* Worth Matravers

Approximately 5½ miles

A peaceful ramble amongst the Purbeck downland and villages, with good coastal and inland views.

Parking
OS Map 195 Ref SY9579. Car park at Kingston village.

Further Exploration
Kingston
This is a trim looking estate village with a gigantic church completed in 1880 and built of Purbeck stone. It has a huge tower which is visible for miles around.

Worth Matravers
A quiet, unspoilt village with steep streets and stone cottages, was once an important centre for quarrying Purbeck stone which supplied many of the churches and cathedrals across England.

*B*ear right onto a lane and, in a short distance, turn right onto a lane waymarked to Hainstout. Descend the lane and bear left onto a track (to Hainstout). Cross a stile and continue along a high grassy ridge to a stile near the cliff edge. Join the coastal footpath and follow the signs towards Chapman's Pool. Once in the valley leading to Champan's Pool, a myriad of paths cross the scrubland eventually leading to the main track. Look for the path ascending the side of the valley and follow this up to the stile at the top. Cross two fields, heading towards a small car park on the left, cross a stile in the wall, over the track and another stile, and follow the footpath signposted to Worth. On reaching a farmyard track, bear left, then right onto a lane to Worth Matravers. Pass the church and small green, bearing left uphill to the pub.

*R*etrace your steps past the church to the children's play area. Pass through the kissing gate and follow the path waymarked to Hill Bottom along the left-hand edge of the field, over a wall stile, past a house on the right, and over a further stile into a cultivated field. Keep to the left-hand edge of the field, heading towards the quarry. Cross a stile in the far corner of the field and remain on the path that skirts around the quarry through a narrow valley, bearing right at a junction towards Afflington Farm. Eventually, you will pass through a gate and emerge from the valley and cross a field with an ancient tumulus to the right, then follow the track on the left up to a farm and a road. Cross the road and follow the waymarked bridleway downhill until you reach a footpath marker post. Bear left, following the yellow arrow, to cross a stile and fields, and head towards a small church. At a road, turn right, then bear left at the Scott Arms pub and return to the car park.

Square & Compass (Whitbread)

This 17th-century building is named after the tools used in stone-quarrying, an important local trade of the past. Enter the old flag-stone corridor to a small servery with two hatchways which serve good ales tapped from the cask. There are two bars, both old-fashioned; one is light and plain, with wall-benches, old tables, glass-fronted cupboards filled with old bottles, and prints and photos of old quarrymen and other characters of the past, on the walls. The larger bar is darker with different styles of tables and chairs around an old stone fireplace. Numerous paintings and photos of the pub in days past decorate the walls, along with a few decorative plates. Outside, there is a seating area which you share with several hungry chickens. Children are welcome.

On draught: Whitbread Pompey Royal and Strong Country, Marston Pedigree, Guinness, Bulmer's Cider. Food: There are snacks such as fresh crab sandwiches, good filled rolls, and various pies and pasties. Food is served at 12-2pm and 7-10pm. Telephone: (0929) 229.

Seatown *to* Symondsbury   Approximately 4½ miles

A strenuous walk in places, through what was once a keen smuggling area, incorporating the West Dorset coastal path, some heathland and old droving routes. There are many fine views inland and along the coast.

Parking

OS Map 193 Ref SY4291
Seatown car park, near
Chideock.

Further Exploration

Symondsbury is a quiet village built almost entirely of the local brown-yellow sandstone. Its 15th-century church has been attractively restored inside.

Chideock is the principle village of a small, fertile vale, with hills on three sides, sloping gently to the sea and scattered with farmsteads and cottages of the yellow sandstone. It contains numerous thatched cottages, a 15th-century church, and an early 19th-century manor house beside an extraordinary ornate Roman Catholic church.

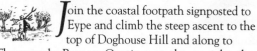

Join the coastal footpath signposted to Eype and climb the steep ascent to the top of Doghouse Hill and along to Thorncombe Beacon. Continue on the coastal path for a short distance until you reach a stile on your left, signposted to Eype Down. Cross, and follow the ridge of the hill to a gate. Proceed along the grassy path to the top of Eype Down and descend, bearing right to a track to quiet lane. Turn left at the lane then, at a bend in the road where the bracken ends, take the path on your left, through the trees, to a stile. Cross, and descend steeply to another stile. Behind the wood, bear left to a further stile and continue uphill to a gate, and eventually to a main road. Turn right and, at the last house, turn left, cross the field, stile and brook. Proceed around the base of the hill before passing through two gates to enter the village of Symondsbury with the pub to your right.

Ilchester Arms (Devenish)

This is a two-storey thatched inn built in 16th-century from local stone. Neatly kept and friendly, there is an open-plan bar with rustic benches and tables, seats in mullioned windows, big inglenook fireplaces, and candlelit tables for dining in a smaller bar. There are tables outside on the quiet lane and in the back garden by a stream and with a view of the church. Children are welcome.

Golden Cap is owned by the National Trust and can be reached by following the coastal footpath to the west of Seatown. A steep climb – it being the highest cliff on England's South Coast at 191 metres – is rewarded with views westwards to Lyme Regis and even to Lizard peninsula on a clear day, and eastwards to Portland.

On draught: John Devenish Dry Hop, Royal Wessex, Newquay Steam lager. Good choice of wines, several by the glass. Food: With a growing reputation for excellent and imaginative food the menu is geared to the seasons and written daily on blackboards or the beams. Emphasis is on locally caught seafood such as crab, lobster, scallops, sole, and even baby shark. Dishes include fresh sardines with a lime sauce (£3.25), thali of fresh vegetables with hot garlic bread (£4.50), and a choice of steaks with a variety of sauces (£8.50). Lunchtime also sees the usual ploughmans and sandwiches. Puddings (£2.25) include Dorset apple cake. Food is served at 12-2pm and 7-9pm (booking advisable at weekends). Not Mondays. Telephone: (0308) 22600.

*L*eaving the inn, follow the road which passes the church and rectory, and soon becomes a track, gradually climbing up behind Colmars Hill – worth a detour for the fine views to the coast and inland towards the Marshwood Vale. At the junction near a barn, it is worth taking the second turning on the right to see a fine example of an ancient droving road. Alternatively, just turn right to a gate and stile, and follow the yellow arrows across fields around the edge of Quarry Hill, down to the main road and into village of Chideock. Turn right on the main road and, at a blue-windowed cottage, follow signposted path back to Seatown.

Woolland *to* Milton Abbas Approximately 7 miles

*Beautiful walk
through deep combes,
across open grassland
and coppiced
woodland. There are
fine views across
meadows and rolling
downland – look out
for buzzards and foxes.*

Parking

OS Map 194 Ref ST7805. Car
park at top of Woolland Hill. One
of the highest hills in Dorset
(261m) with fine views across
the Blackmore Vale into North
Dorset and Wiltshire.

Further Exploration

Milton Abbas is one of
England's most picturesque
villages. It grew up beside an
ancient monastery founded by
Athelstan in AD933 on the site
of the present Abbey. Lord
Milton, who owned the mansion
near the Abbey in 1774, could
not bear the village on his
doorstep so he had it removed
and rebuilt in its present
location. The church was built
using stone and timber from the
Abbey's tithe barn.

Milton Abbey dates from the
14th century and stands in front
of a hill surmounted by the
Norman St Catherine's Chapel.

*T*ake the lane towards Milton Abbas,
go straight on at the next road
junction and then take the blue-arrowed
bridleway on the right. Cross the meadow down to a
gateway into the wood, and follow the bridleway
through the woods into Heath Bolton, a deep combe.
Join the private lane and continue to a farm and
turning for Winterbourne Haighton on the left. Bear
left and follow the established track up to a gate.
Follow the blue arrow away from the track onto a
grassy path, towards a small woodland. Do not enter
the woodland, but bear right before passing through a
gate on the left, and reaching the road. Turn left
along the road and then take a bridleway on the right.
Follow this down into the village of Milton Abbas.

*F*rom the inn, walk down the main
street, lined with 18th-century
thatched cottages. At the lake, bear right
at the junction. After a short distance, follow a
bridleway beside a thatched cottage, to Milton Abbey
and the school. Keep to the path at the rear of the
Abbey, passing behind the school grounds onto a
small lane. Bear left and continue in front of the
school. Take the bridleway (blue-arrow) on the right
up into the woods and follow this well-defined path
up to Bulbarrow Farm and a tarmac drive. On
reaching the lane, bear right and follow back to the
car park.

Hambro Arms (Devenish)

The thatched and whitewashed appearance of this 18th-century pub completes the picturesque scene of a fine village street. The cosy interior evokes an air of 'olde worlde' charm; the comfortable lounge has an open fire and round tables, and the dining room has various old tables and a large inglenook. Walls are adorned with early prints and a collection of pub water jugs. A few tables at the front of the pub offer good views down the village street, and there is a small terrace with tables to one side.

On draught: Royal Wessex Bitter, John Devenish Dry Hop. Food: Bar food includes good snacks at lunchtime with imaginative ploughmans (£2.95) using Stilton, Dorset paté, Chedder or roast beef, homemade soup (£1.95), quiche and salad (£4.25). Specials include tagliatelle with smoked salmon and cream sauce (£4.25), pork curry and calves liver with lemon (£6.25). Puddings are £1.95. Sunday carvery costs £8.95, but you will need to book. Food is served at 12-2pm and 7-9.30pm (Sunday 7-8.30pm). Telephone: (0258) 880233.

Park Farm Museum – on Bulbarrow Road – displays old village photographs, documents and bygones, and there are many different farm animals on show. Telephone: (0258) 880216.

Rare Poultry, Pig and Plant Centre, Long Ash Farm, is located next to the lake at the bottom of the village. Telephone: (0258) 880447.

Alresford *to* Ovington

Approximately 6½ miles

A tranquil ramble beside two fine chalk streams, through idyllic thatched villages and across open undulating farmland. Look out for herons, kingfishers, ducks and the trout swimming in the clear water.

Parking

OS Map 185 Ref SU5832
Alresford station car park, or in Broad Street.

Further Exploration

Alresford is one of Hampshire's most picturesque towns with its wide Broad Street lined with Georgian houses, speciality shops and pubs. In medieval days, Alresford was an important wool town in which the 14th-century fulling mill played a major role. Broad Street leads down to a medieval causeway (new road) that was built to create Alresford Lake – a delightful reed-fringed sheet of water, and an important refuge for wildfowl. The town is also important for watercress cultivation; large areas close to the River Itchen are ideal for producing this salad crop. Hampshire supplies over half the country's watercress.

*F*rom the car park, head towards the town centre and Broad Street, a wide main street flanked with lime trees and colour-washed Georgian houses and shops. At the bottom, bear left and go down 'Mill Hill' towards the river. Turn left at a green fingerpost, waymarked 'Wayfarers Walk - Inkpen Beacons 36'. This established footpath follows the River Arle to a quiet lane. Cross this and follow the wide track, to a junction where you bear left, cross a stream and continue up to an isolated cottage. Here, take the track off to the left through the wood and across arable land towards Winchester, passing isolated cottages and a farm before reaching a B-road. Turn right towards Itchen Stoke until you reach the church. There, cross the B-road and take the lane beside the small village green, down to the River Itchen and over a small footbridge. Continue along a short stretch of this beautiful river bank before crossing the bridge, and joining the pub driveway with pub to the right.

Bush Inn (Free House)

This fine old rose-covered pub is tucked away in the peace and quiet of the Itchen valley beside the river. Inside, the softly-lit bars are adorned with copper pans, old hunting prints, and giant antique bellows beside the large open fire, and are furnished with high-backed settles, elm tables, pews and old wooden chairs. A very pleasant, sheltered garden offers a relaxing place for a drink and is safe for children, who are allowed in the eating area (lunchtimes) and in the restaurant.

On draught: Gales HSB, Flower's Original, Whitbread Strong Country, Hall & Woodhouse Tanglefoot, Guinness, Stella Artois. There is also a fine range of country wines available by the glass. Food: A good selection of home-cooked food includes soup (£1), ploughmans (from £3), lamb casserole (£5.95), and lemon sole (£7.95). Food is served at 12-2pm and 7-10pm. Telephone: (0962) 732764.

*L*eave the pub, bear right at the lane, cross the bridge and continue uphill, passing Ovington church and the walled garden of Ovington House. Reaching the point where the driveway to the house leaves the lane, take the waymarked footpath on left and follow it around the edge of a field, entering a small wood before reaching a large lay-by beside the A31. Turn left, cross the road, and continue along the edge of a field. At a junction of fields, bear right, then immediately left – this time with the field edge to the left – and follow the track. Reaching a lane, bear left past the old thatched post office and pub, and take the turning off to your right into Tichborne Park. Cross the river, pass some cottages on the left and then bear left at a bend to follow a gravel track, with the River Itchen away to the left. At the entrance to Vemal Farm, bear right over the stile, and walk along the waymarked path towards Alresford. Cross further stiles to join the B-road, turn left over the main road, and follow the road back into Alresford town centre.

Well worth a visit is the mid-Hants Railway, also known as the Watercress Line as it was once the major despatch point for watercress. The line, which linked Alton and Winchester, has been restored and is run by enthusiasts between Alresford and Alton. In summer months, steam trains run regularly, visiting four stations on its journey.

Itchen Stoke has an interesting, though redundant, church built in 1866 to resemble La Saint Chapelle in Paris; it is beautifully decorated and has some fine stained glass.

River Itchen is one of the finest unspoilt chalk streams in Europe, with a naturally breeding population of brown and rainbow trout. It also supports a good birdlife, namely grebes, duck, herons and species of warblers.

Walbury Hill *to* Vernham Street

Approximately 6 miles

This walk takes you across the high downs surrounding the village of Combe, and affords spectacular views across the countryside. Some of the hills are very steep and stout footwear is advised.

Parking

OS Map 174 Ref SU3861
Gravel and grass car park to the east of Walbury Hill, where the bridleways cross.

Further Exploration

The hills that cradle Combe are typical chalk downland with its associated flora and fauna including cowslips, orchids and blue butterflies. Wild strawberries grow on shaded banks and the open fields support many hares. The only village passed on this route is Linkenholt which has many interesting flint and brick buildings and a beautiful clock tower with a copper roof.

 *F*rom the car park, several paths are signposted. Take the path to the south which leads downhill across grazing land. On reaching a stony track, go to the left (away from the farm) and follow this path steeply uphill between banks of wild flowers, to come out among arable fields and eventually to an unclassified metalled road, where you turn right. A short distance past the radio mast on your left, take the next track on the right which cuts back through the fields and on past a beautiful valley and then through woodland. On reaching a metalled road, follow the sign to Linkenholt (straight ahead). At Linkenholt, take the right fork towards Vernham Street, past the village post office and on for about ½ mile to the pub.

Boot (Free House)

This 15th-century inn is of brick-and-flint construction and has a lovely thatched roof and what is probably the most unusual pub sign in the country. There are two cosy bars, both low-beamed with white-panelled walls, and one with a large open fireplace and the other with a dart board. There is also a spacious conservatory, in which children are welcome, and a small room for private or family use. The large lawn has plenty of tables, chairs and picnic benches.

On draught: Marston Pedigree and Burton, Wadworth 6X, Hall & Woodhouse Badger Best, Hook Norton Old Hookey, Guinness, Carlsberg Pils and Export, Strongbow cider. Food : Homemade meals include chicken and chips (£4.20), fisherman's platter (£4.95), various vegetarian meals (£3.50), steak (£6.80), various ploughmans (£3.75) and sandwiches (from £1.25). Desserts include locally made ice cream (£1.25), apple crumble (£1.60), and Death by Chocolate (£2.20). Food is served at 12-2pm and 7-9.30pm (not Mondays or Sunday evenings). Telephone: (026487) 213.

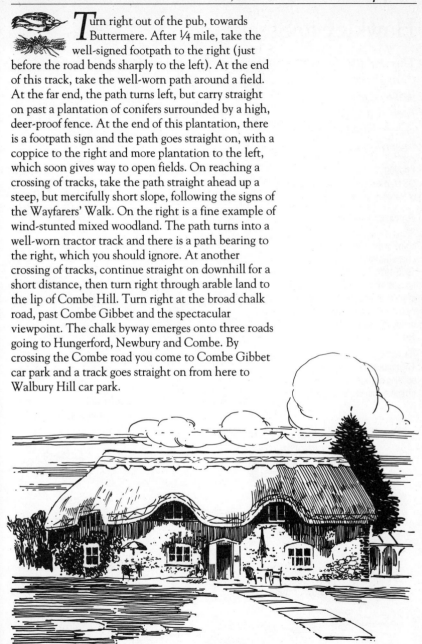

*T*urn right out of the pub, towards Buttermere. After ¼ mile, take the well-signed footpath to the right (just before the road bends sharply to the left). At the end of this track, take the well-worn path around a field. At the far end, the path turns left, but carry straight on past a plantation of conifers surrounded by a high, deer-proof fence. At the end of this plantation, there is a footpath sign and the path goes straight on, with a coppice to the right and more plantation to the left, which soon gives way to open fields. On reaching a crossing of tracks, take the path straight ahead up a steep, but mercifully short slope, following the signs of the Wayfarers' Walk. On the right is a fine example of wind-stunted mixed woodland. The path turns into a well-worn tractor track and there is a path bearing to the right, which you should ignore. At another crossing of tracks, continue straight on downhill for a short distance, then turn right through arable land to the lip of Combe Hill. Turn right at the broad chalk road, past Combe Gibbet and the spectacular viewpoint. The chalk byway emerges onto three roads going to Hungerford, Newbury and Combe. By crossing the Combe road you come to Combe Gibbet car park and a track goes straight on from here to Walbury Hill car park.

Hawkley *to* Steep

Approximately 6 miles

This undulating walk through beech hangers, across pasture and farmland, is especially beautiful in spring.

Parking
OS Map 197 Ref SU7429 Edge of Hawkley Green

Further Exploration
Steep is known as being the home of the First World War poet Edward Thomas, from 1906-1916. He lived in three houses whilst in the village, one of which is Berryfield Cottage, next to Ashford Chace. He died during the Battle of Arras in 1917.

Ashford Chace
The gardens of this large building are open to the public on some summer Sundays.

From Hawkley church take the no through road southwards. As the road heads left downhill, bear right and soon cross a stile on the left. Follow the path downhill to another stile, and keep to the left-hand edge of the field. Cross the small stream and a further stile, to follow the path along the edge of the woodland, eventually bearing right up a steep hill to a stile. Follow the path and bear left to pass through a gate and join another path. Turn right and head uphill to a road. Turn right, then left up a gravel track. On the heavily wooded ridge, bear left at a junction, then take the second path on the right through a small gate downhill to a lane. Turn left to another lane, and keep left before taking the waymarked path on your right next to a driveway. Cross three stiles, and bear right across a field. Turn left over a stile, soon to cross another stile, and follow the left-hand edge of the field to a stile. Cross and follow the waymarked path to the left of some old farm buildings, into woodland. When you meet another track, turn left across a stile, go uphill over the next stile and head across the field towards a stile in the fence on the left. Cross, and when you reach a narrow lane, turn right. At a sharp left-hand bend, turn right, cross a stream and continue up to the pub on the right.

Harrow (Whitbread)

 This is a very pretty two-storey, brick and
tiled inn whose two separate bars are
simply furnished with wooden tables and
benches, tiled floors, huge log fires and stripped pine
wall boards. The walls are adorned with old prints of
local characters and the cricket team, and there are
also a few bookshelves crammed with reading
material. Both bars are served from small hatches with
beer dispensed straight from the cask. Outside, sturdy
tables and benches crowd the front area, and there is a
colourful garden at the back. Children are not allowed
inside.

On draught: Flower's Original, Strong Country,
Boddingtons Best. Food: Superb, home-cooked meals
are served in very generous portions, and include soup
(£1.70), ploughmans (£2.70), sandwiches (from
£1.10), lasagne (£4), scotch eggs (£1) and huge salads
(£5). Food is served at 12-2pm and 6.30-10pm.
Telephone: (0730) 62685.

*T*urn right out of the pub, then right
again at a road. Follow this uphill to
Steep church, across a small playing field
into woodland. Emerging from this, cross a stile and
keep to the left-hand edge of the field to a road. Bear
right and, at a corner near a mill house, take the path
on the left, which soon joins another path. Keep left
to join another track, and bear right, following this up
to a gateway and a lane, with Ashford Chace to the
left. Turn right, then almost immediately left onto a
waymarked path uphill into the hangers and bear
right on the main ridge track. Cross a stile and follow
the good path down through the beautiful beech trees
to a lane near Middle Oakshott Farms. Cross over
into pasture land, keeping to the path, and when the
grass track bends right uphill, keep left near the
stream. Cross the planks over the stream and follow
the path below the wood, eventually rejoining the
outward route at the edge of the pasture land. Bear
left at the fence, cross a stile, and retrace your steps
back to the green and your car.

Buriton *to* Chalton
Approximately 6½ miles

A peaceful walk along Downland tracks and through mixed forest.

Parking
OS Map 197 Ref SU7319
Forestry Commission car park south of Buriton village.

Further Exploration
Chalton
This small village nestling amongst the Downs has two notable buildings either side of its sloping stretch of green; a partly 13th-century church and the Red Lion. Close to the church is its former rectory, a partly medieval building. Also in the village are a number of Victorian cottages.

Cross the lane away from the forest following the South Downs Way, pass Dean Barn and join a rough track which takes you over two hills, passing a farm and barns. Where the road bears left, take the bridleway on the right along the edge of a small nature reserve. Pass through a gate and follow the established path up through the wood. At a junction of tracks, keep straight and then bear right on the edge of the wood and follow the wide clearing. Where this bends right downhill, bear left through a gate and follow the path over the brow of a hill to join a quiet country lane. Turn right and follow the road, shortly taking a gravel track straight ahead, which leads downhill, with Ditcham House (school) on the right. Remain on this track passing some cottages, woodland and open fields, down to a road at Woodcroft Farm. Cross the road, following the waymarked path through a farmyard and over a railway footbridge. At a quiet lane, bear left, then right near a house, crossing a stile to follow the footpath up a steep rise. Cross a further stile and bear diagonally left across an arable field towards a telegraph pole. At a stile, bear right onto a road down into the village of Chalton. At a road junction, turn left to the pub, which lies opposite the church.

Return to the road junction and follow the waymarked path between cottages past the farm buildings, through a gate and along the edge of a field. Near the pylons, bear left across an arable field to the field edge and a stile leading into the forest. A short, narrow path soon leads onto a broader one, which you follow to the first junction, where you bear left. At a major junction, keep straight and follow the track up into the woodland. Follow the path along a ridge over a junction with a horse trail, and eventually down to a gateway and the car park.

Red Lion (Gales)

This is the oldest pub in Hampshire, dating back to 1147, and was first built to serve the stonemasons working on the church. It is an attractive timbered and thatched pub and overlooks the South Downs. The main bar is heavily beamed and panelled, and its ancient inglenook fireplace has an unusual frieze of threepenny bits set into its beam. Wooden settles and simple tables and chairs provide comfortable seating. A further bar is also beamed, carpeted, and warmed by a large open fire. A more modern extension contains a dining room, and there is a terraced beer garden. Children are welcome in the dining area and the garden.

On draught: Gales BBB, HSB, XXXXX (winter brew). Food: Good home-cooked food ranges from ploughmans (£1.40) plaice and chips(£3), pizza(£4.25) and grilled gammon (£4.25). Food is served at 12-2.30pm and 7-10pm. Telephone: (0705) 592246.

Goodworth Clatford *to* Testcombe

Approximately 6 miles

A riverside walk along the Anton and Test valleys through gently undulating farmland.

Parking

OS Map 185 Ref SU3642 by the church.

Further Exploration

The Test valley abounds in picturesque villages, of which Stockbridge, Wherwell and Longparish are good examples. Winchester, with its great cathedral, is a delightful old city and to the west of Andover is the Hawk Conservancy at Weyhill, devoted to birds of prey.

Walk through the village to a footpath on your left, just past Fishing Cottage. Follow the footpath uphill to emerge into a field, with the River Anton on your right. Follow the river bank towards the sewage works. Just before you reach a gate, turn right to cross a wooden footbridge into a watermeadow, turning right to retrace your steps along the opposite bank, but soon turning left to cross the field, following the line of the fence. Through a gate, turn left onto a bridleway to a belt of trees which marks the start of an abandoned railway cutting. Climb up the field on your right, skirting its edge until you reach a broader path at the top, turning left to walk along the ridge of the field to emerge into a steep, narrow lane opposite Fullerton Manor. Turn left downhill to the A3057. Alternatively, you can continue on the bridlepath – although it is not a public right of way, and is often used by shooting parties. The path leads round to the right in front of an old bridge to join the lane, where you turn left to reach the A3057. Turn right on to the main road and continue for 1/4 mile to the pub.

Mayfly (Whitbread)

This pub has an idyllic location, right on the bank of the River Test – Hampshire's most famous trout fishing river – below an old arched bridge. Chairs and tables line its waterfront terrace and inside are three spacious bar areas with a conservatory overlooking the river. Its location and excellent buffet bar make this pub a very popular meeting place, especially in the summer. Children are allowed in away from the bar.

On draught: Best, Strong Country, Flower's Original, Stella Artois, Heineken, Strongbow cider. Food: The menu consists largely of a range of very good cold meats with a wide choice of salads. There is usually also a hot dish of the day. Prices range from around £2.50 to £4.20. Food is served at 12-2pm and 7-9pm. Telephone: (0264) 860283.

*O*n leaving the pub, cross the bridge, then turn left towards Chilbolton. Walk along this pretty, wooded lane for about ½ mile until you see on your left a little fenced square of grass with a garden seat overlooking the River Test. A waymarked footpath (green arrow on white background) leads between high fences to a playing field. Cross by the sports hut to a track leading to your left and pass an old thatched cottage onto common land. Keep right around the common, following the green arrows, across a bridge and on across the common to two more footbridges which bring you out on to a country lane. Turn left and very soon, take the footpath on your right leading up a steep bank to two stiles. Take the left-hand stile and, keeping the hedge on your left, walk round the edge of the field until you reach the very top. Here, take the path on your right leading between tall hedges, and follow it along until it bends left downhill through some bushes and across a neck of the field below to a gate on to the main road. Cross over to the field path opposite and walk along the edge of the field to a gate which leads you back on to the path alongside the River Anton. Retrace your steps past the sewage works to Goodworth Clatford.

Breamore *to* Whitsbury

Approximately 5 miles

A gentle ramble through rolling farmland and peaceful mixed woodland on good tracks.

Parking
OS Map 184 Ref SU1518
Breamore Church.

Further Exploration
Breamore House
This fine manor house was built around 1583 and contains a magnificent collection of paintings, china and tapestries. There is also a Countryside & Carriage Museum with good examples of coaches and steam engines, and reconstructed workshops and other displays show how people lived, worked and travelled over a century ago. Telephone: (0725) 22468.

Walk back down the driveway of Breamore House to a quiet lane, bear right and follow the lane into Upper Street. Take the turning on the right by a letter box. The lane becomes a track just past a thatched cottage, and gradually rises uphill. Keep straight until you reach a stile. Cross and follow the waymarked path downhill, pass through a metal gate, cross a wide track, go through another gate, and follow the path at the edge of the field uphill towards a wood. Once in the wood, at a junction with another track, bear right and soon follow the path between paddocks and woodland. On reaching a bungalow, bear left and follow a track to Whitsbury church. Enter the churchyard and pass through the gate to the left of the church. Cross the field down to another gate. Shortly, on reaching the lane in the village, bear right for the pub.

Turn right out of the pub and follow the quiet lane up through the village to Whitsbury Stud, home of the 1988 Grand National winner, 'Rhyme and Reason'. Here, take the waymarked path on right around the back of the stables, along the edge of the paddocks. Keep to this wide bridleway – in the woodland on the right, you can see the ramparts of Whitsbury Iron Age Fort; excavations have revealed the outline of a circular timber house. Go downhill, cross the stile at the bottom and continue uphill through a small wood. Cross the stile at the top and bear right along a wide track with woodland ahead on the right. In a short distance, a detour into this woodland reveals the unusual Mizmaze – a cobweb-like turf maze 87 feet across, surrounded by yew trees and believed to be Anglo-Saxon in origin. Return to the main path and keep to this, through Breamore wood, to emerge beside the impressive Breamore House. Walk down the drive and bear left back to the church and car.

Cartwheel (Free House)

Located in the peaceful village of Whitsbury, the Cartwheel is a homely country pub. Originally two cottages, the brick building has been extended to the rear and now offers a main bar with a huge, warming log fire with cushioned wall-seating and sturdy benches and tables. Beyond this is the bar area and further tables, a games room and a cosy dining area. A horse-racing theme runs through the pub with some interesting prints and photographs of the local winners on the walls. Outside, a good garden has a barbecue area and children's play area. No children under 14 are allowed inside.

On draught: Wadworth 6X, Wiltshire Old Grumble, Ringwood Fortyniner, Whitbread Pompey Royal, Wethered Winter Royal, Stella Artois, Fosters, Murphy's Stout. Food: A good range of bar food includes lasagne (£3.85), steak and kidney pudding (£4.50), lemon sole (£7), smoked salmon quiche (£3.75), jacket potatoes with 13 choices of fillings (from £2.50), and sandwiches (from £1.25). Desserts include bread and butter pudding and profiteroles. Food is served at 12-2pm and 7-10pm. Telephone: (07253) 362.

Swallowcliffe Down *to* Ebbesbourne Wake

Approximately 6 miles

Chalk downland and valley walk incorporating open meadows and ancient ox droving routes, affording outstanding views into the heart of Wiltshire on one side, and across Ebble Valley on the other. There is an abundance of wild flowers, notably wild thyme, and wildlife such as hares, skylarks, red-legged partridges and pheasants.

Parking
OS Map 184 Ref ST9625 Top of Swallowcliffe/Middle Downs – an old ox drove off a country lane.

Walk westwards along the ox drove towards White Sheet Hill. Shortly after you emerge from the trees, follow a path to your left, waymarked with a blue arrow. With a track merging from the right, follow the footpath on your left (blue arrow). This path keeps to the edge of the wood, downhill, through a gate and on to a track, which brings you down to Norington, a large medieval-looking manor house. Cross the concrete drive and pass between the farm outbuildings, bearing right at a fence, towards the front of the house. Cross the stile next to the fuel pump and continue across the grazing land towards some houses. After the next stile and driveway, follow the footpath beside a stream, towards Alvediston church. Cross the lane and keep to the waymarked path beside the river, past both the church and the rectory, and through a gate. Cross the field and pass through another gate on to a track and continue past the cottages at West End. Reaching a lane, cross the bridge and follow the lane signposted to Ebbesborne Wake. At a fork in the lane, bear left, then at a path by some white railings, head off to the right, up to the church and into the main village street, bearing right.

The Horseshoe (Free House)

 This attractive country pub has a pleasant, well-kept garden with numerous picnic benches which overlook the quiet, steep-sided Ebble valley. Inside, a central serving bar serves two rooms; the snug, a tiny room with a fireplace, wooden tables and chairs, and prints and curiosities on the walls; and the public bar with beams, lanterns, a vast collection of farm tools and a large open fire. A further room with a wood-burning stove, houses the small, neat restaurant. Children are welcome in the eating areas, and garden is very safe for youngsters.

On draught: Bunces, Wadworth 6X, Ringwood Best, Adnams Broadside, Guinness, Carlsberg. Food: Simple bar food includes home-made soup (£1.20), ploughmans (from £2.50), and sandwiches (from £1.30). A few hot dishes are also available. Puddings are home-made and include fruit pies and crumbles (£1.50). An excellent Sunday lunch consists of three courses for £5.95. Bar food is served at 12-2pm. The restaurant is open 7-9.30pm and for Sunday lunch (booking essential). Telephone: (0722) 780474.

*T*urn right out of the pub, then turn left downhill past some thatched cottages. At a left-hand bend, take the path to your right, crossing a small footbridge. Cross a stile on your left and keep left, crossing the field diagonally up to a stile in the hedge (not immediately visible). Turn left on the lane, then right onto a waymarked path next to a house. Continue uphill, through a gate to an arable field and then through a gate on your right and across another field. Pass through another gate and head straight down the side of the valley and through a gate beside a small wood. Follow the established track up through the centre of the valley, then bear right through the thicket up to the valley head. Emerging from the thicket, bear left through gate on to an established track. Turn left again and follow this track along the edge of two fields before crossing a stile to join the old ox drove. Keep left and follow the path back to the car.

Farley *to* Pitton

Approximately 4½ miles

A peaceful walk across pasture and arable land with short mature woodland stretches, offering views across gently rolling rural landscape.

Parking

OS Map 184 Ref SU2229 Farley church.

Further Exploration

Farley church and the attractive almshouses opposite (Farley Hospital), were built around 1680 and are attributed to Sir Christopher Wren. The brick church is unusual for the period and contains none of the elaborate decoration found in many of Wren's London churches, but its simplicity fits the rural setting. The hospital opposite was built around the same time as Chelsea hospital for soldiers in London, also designed by Wren.

From Farley church, follow the lane westwards, passing a cricket ground on your right. On reaching a junction, bear left, keeping to a quiet lane. At the end of a line of houses on your right, cross the stile waymarked to Clarendon and cross two fields, another stile and then bear right on to an established track. Remain on this through mature mixed woodland until you reach a junction of paths. Bear left and then, just before reaching the lane, cross a stile on your right and cross the field diagonally to the base of the hill, keeping the house to your left. Keep to the path through the edge of the woodland, before joining another track. Turn right, passing a tennis court and village hall into the lane. The pub lies to the left, across the lane.

Silver Plough (Free House)

 This large, whitewashed converted farmhouse offers a warm welcome and a convivial atmosphere in which to enjoy some excellent food and ale. The main front bar is large with a number of red velvet-cushioned antique wooden settles and some oak tables. Black beams are adorned with a collection of antique boot-warmers and stretchers, pewter and china tankards, brass and copper jugs, glass rolling pins, and other unusual ornaments. The back bar is smaller with high-backed settles. Both bars contain some impressive paintings and prints. There is also a large restaurant off the main bar where children are welcome, and a skittle alley. The garden at the front is neat and quiet with numerous picnic tables.

On draught: Wadworth 6X, Courage Best and Directors, Gales Best, Guinness, Heineken. Food: This is the main attraction here and is excellent. Imaginative dishes are available (see changing blackboard menu) as well as substantial bar snacks at lunchtimes, including a selection of cheese ploughmans (£3.50), pasta dishes (from £4.95), fresh mussels (£4.50) and more substantial dishes such as lamb's liver or salmon with basil sauce. Desserts are imaginative. Food is served at 12-2pm and 7-10pm. Telephone: (072272) 266.

*F*rom the pub, turn right down the lane, right again at the crossroads and walk to the church. There, take the tarmaced footpath on the right, cross the lane and continue uphill, crossing two stiles and an open field. Cross over the farm driveway with the farm to your left and keep on the track to the coniferous woodland ahead. On entering the wooded area, bear right following the green arrow on a tree. Keep to this main path, ignoring all other paths until you reach a gravelled track. Bear right and follow this back to Farley village.

Harting Down *to* Hooksway

Approximately 6½ miles

A beautiful walk along the South Downs Way, offering panoramic views across Sussex, and some quiet woodland paths.

Parking

OS Map 197 Ref SU7918. Large car park on top of Harting Down, off B2141.

Take the South Downs Way on the right heading east. Keep to this path to a multi-sign oak post. Climb straight up to the top of Beacon Hill. Carry straight on downhill and through a field, then bear right along the headland path, keeping on the ridge. Keep straight on at the next junction and soon the path bends to the left and goes between first a hedge and the woods, and then two fields. On reaching a track, bear left, soon turning right along a broad track with Burton farm to the right. On joining a second path, take the lower path on the right and then bear right again onto another signposted path. This path keeps straight on to a broad track, which leads you down to Hooksway and the pub.

Royal Oak (Free House)

Nestling in a hollow within the Downs, at the end of a lane, this rustic pub is a welcome sight after the breezy walk across the top of the Downs. Inside, there are two open fires and rough flagstones in its two simply furnished bars. Low ceilings with a few beams, and stools around the bar, provide a welcoming atmosphere in which to enjoy a good meal. The garden has sturdy picnic benches and there is a climbing frame for children, who are also welcome inside.

On draught: Ballards Best, Gibbs Mew Bishop's Tipple, Gales HSB, Ruddles Best, Ringwood Old Thumper, Guinness. Food: A varied menu includes ploughmans (from £2.80), jacket potatoes (from £2.40), venison pie (£4.25), chilli (£3.85) and tagliatelle (£3.85). Desserts include banoffi pie, cheesecake and gateau (all at £1.80). Food is served at 12-2pm and 7-9.30pm. The restaurant also serves afternoon cream teas. Telephone: (024359) 257.

*T*urn right out of the pub and follow the metalled lane uphill. Before reaching the top, bear right onto a broad track and at a T-junction, turn right. Before a bungalow on the left, leave the track, cross a stile on the left and follow the waymarked path across a field by a fence, and then join a metalled track, bearing right. Keep right, with the Telegraph House on your left, and once past the large house, take the path on the right up to a gate. Follow the waymarked path for about ¼ mile and, just before the end of the field on the right, bear left (signposted) downhill into woodland. At the bottom of the hill, go straight on at a junction and head uphill, bearing right at the top. In a short distance, take the path waymarked on the right and, at the end of the woods, bear left onto an arrowed path between woodland and open grassland. Bear left at a junction of paths. With the road in sight, turn right over a stile into the car park.

Firle Beacon *to* Alciston

Approximately 6 miles

Downland walk following the South Downs Way with fine views over the Sussex Weald into Kent, of rolling downs and the magnificent coastline.

Parking

OS Map 198 Ref TQ468059
Viewpoint near Firle Beacon.

Further Exploration

Alciston has been known as the forgotten village since its population fled before the ravages of the Black Death, leaving a 13th-century church and 14th-century Alciston Court. Of particular note is the 170ft tithe barn, said to be the longest in the country. There is a mediaeval dovecote near the church. On Good Friday, traditional village skipping takes place at the Rose Cottage Inn.

Charleston Farmhouse

This former home of Clive and Vanessa Bell was an important artistic focus for the artists and writers of the 'Bloomsbury Group'. Charleston became a habitation of genius and talent; constant visitors included Virginia and Leonard Woolf, Duncan Grant, TS Eliot, EM Forster, Roger Fry and Lytton Strachey. Today, Charleston remains a remarkable monument to the creative achievements of Bell, Grant and other artists; the last surviving complete example of their domestic decorative work anywhere in the world. Telephone: (032183) 265.

*F*ollow the signpost eastwards for the South Downs Way. The wide, grassy downland path leads up to Firle Beacon and past a farm, another car park, and up onto Bostal Hill where various tumuli are visible on the ground. Where the path meets a gate and a track running south (at end of fencing), bear diagonally right towards the edge of the Downs. Locate a stile, cross and follow path off the edge of the Downs, heading towards Alciston. At the metalled road, follow for ¼ mile to the pub.

*T*urn left out of the pub and follow the road until, before reaching main road, you reach and cross a stile on your left, located at the rear of a small drive. Follow arrows across a small stream to a lane, turn left and then right, and follow the concrete driveway. Continue straight past the cottage through the gates, reaching a driveway and sign for Charleston Farmhouse. Pass in front of the house and remain on marked footpaths and stiles, passing beneath Firle Tower on your right, to join a track beside two cottages. Cross the stile immediately ahead and cross Firle Park, following the arrows. Pass in front of Firle House and through the gate onto a road into Firle village. Bear left at the main lane, past the church, then continue straight on through a farm and follow the footpath up along the edge of Firle Plantation (steep ascent) to rejoin the South Downs Way a short distance from the car park.

Rose Cottage (Free House)

Nestling at the base of the South Downs, this well-run little cottage has cosy bars adorned with artefacts such as harnesses, traps, thatcher blades and other ironware. A few stuffed birds, plus a real one – a talking parrot – wheel-backed chairs, red leatherette seats, and open fires, combine to create a relaxed atmosphere. Outside, there is plenty of seating by the wistaria, and a small paddock with chickens, a goat and a duckpond. Walkers are very welcome and children are allowed in the eating area and restaurant.

On draught: Harvey Best, Ruddles Best. Food: Generous helpings of good simple food include soup (from £1.25), brie and asparagus quiche (£2.95), rabbit pie (£2.95), and curried nut loaf (£3.25). Food is served at 12-2pm and 7-10pm.
Telephone: (0323) 870377.

Firle
Once a feudal village, Firle is dominated by Firle Place. Owned by the Gage family since 15th-century, it houses a magnificent collection of Sèvres porcelain, fine English and French furniture and galleries containing paintings by Van Dyck, Gainsborough and Reynolds. St Peter's church in the village dates from 14th-century although the north door is Norman and records of vicars of Firle go as far back as 1197. Telephone: (079159) 335.

Seven Sisters Country Park *to* Litlington

Approximately 4 miles

Along the South Downs Way there are fine views of the Downs, across the meandering Cuckmere river and towards the sea. The return brings you along the Cuckmere Valley which is rich in wildlife.

Parking

OS Map 199 Ref TV5199. Car park beside A259, opposite the Living World and Interpretation Centre.

*T*urn right uphill on the pavement before crossing over to follow the waymarked South Downs Way between two buildings. Cross a stile and climb uphill across the field to a further stile. Follow the wide path through Friston Forest, down wooden steps into the peaceful hamlet of Westdean. Follow the yellow arrows and acorn signs for the South Downs Way, and gradually climb out of the village, bearing left back into the forest along a wide grassy path. Cross a stile and head downhill towards Charleston Manor on the left. Keep to the South Downs Way signs and cross another stile to follow the left-hand edge of the field uphill. You will soon follow the path through fields downhill to Litlington nestling beside the River Cuckmere. Enter the village via a stile, bearing left down a track, and bear right on the quiet lane to the pub.

Plough & Harrow (Free House)

This is a fine old inn with good views of the Cuckmere Valley and nearby Alfriston from the garden, where there are a number of rustic seats and an aviary. The inn is an attractive building, the interior being beamed and carpeted, with numerous tables surrounded by old barrel seats plus a few old settles. Off the large main bar is the original front bar with comfortable seating, and decorated with a few mirrors on the walls. Beyond the main bar is a small, cosy dining area, with pictures and models following a theme of steam railways. Children are welcome in the restaurant area, and there is a children's bar serving soft drinks in summer.

On draught: Harvey Best, Hall & Woodhouse Badger Best, Adnams Southwold, Young's Special, guest beers, Guinness, Stella Artois, Carlsberg. Food: There is a good range of standard bar snacks from a printed menu, including soup (£1.95), omelettes (from £3), ploughmans (from £2.85), lasagne (£4.30), sandwiches (from £1.35), steak and kidney pie (£4.40), and steaks (from £6.75). Food is served at 12-2pm and 7-10pm. Telephone: (0323) 870632.

*B*ear right out of the pub and walk down the lane, soon taking the path on the right at end of village to the bridge over the River Cuckmere. Do not cross the bridge, but bear left along the footpath on the river's left bank. At the main road, cross onto the footpath, turn left and follow it down the road back to the car park. If you wish to visit the ancient village of Alfriston (a mile further on from the pub) before returning back to the car, bear left up the lane past the church, and follow the South Downs Way signs on the left into meadowland, across a couple of fields, and over the white bridge into the village. On returning, retrace your steps over the bridge, and take the footpath beside the river to join the main route.

Further Exploration

The Living World & Interpretation Centre
This is a diverse and entertaining exhibition of living exotic and native creatures housed in a beautiful flint barn. The interpretation centre also houses an information centre and historical exhibits from the area. Open daily. Telephone: (0323) 870100.

Westdean
This is a peaceful hamlet, with a pretty duckpond and fine Norman church. It is said King Alfred once had a palace here.

Alfriston
England's prettiest Downland village has timbered houses, winding streets and a spreading chestnut tree in the village square. Next to the beautiful village green is the 13th-century 'Cathedral of the Downs' and beside this stands the Old Clergy House' (National Trust) – a timbered and thatched priest's house and a fine example of medieval architecture. Telephone: (0323) 870001.

Wilmington Priory
Built by Benedictine monks, this houses an agricultural museum and is a fine vantage point to view the 'Long Man of Wilmington'– a 200-foot carving in the chalk downland, probably neolithic in origin and extensively restored at the end of the 19th century.

Burwash *to* Oxley's Green — Approximately 6 miles

A hill and vale walk through the old Wealden iron industry landscape, with pretty views across wooded valleys, towards hill-top villages.

Parking

OS Map 199 Ref TQ6724. Village car park.

Further Exploration

At 197m, Brightling Down is the highest point in the area and is the place to find Mad Jack Fuller's Folly, one of four built by the ironmaster, squire and former MP for Lewes, who died in 1834. The second is a lead-covered Dome Pagoda at Brightling Park, and there is a 40ft high Sugar Loaf at nearby Dallington, the result of a bet Fuller had with some friends. He claimed that he could see the spire of Dallington church from his home, but lost. So he built a replica of the spire at Woods Corner, which was within sight of his house.

*T*he walk begins at the churchyard, which is claimed to have the oldest cast-iron grave slab in the country. Follow the footpath behind the church and over two stiles before gradually bearing right towards the old pond, over two more stiles, through a gate and over yet another stile. From here, stiles are marked with a yellow arrow and a 'Landowners' badge, so follow these across the fields and the River Dodwell, until you reach a house, then follow the tarmac drive on its right to join a lane. Turn right here, and then take the first left-hand road, which is signposted to Sockernash Manor. When you reach this fine, 17th-century brick and timber-frame building, take the bridleway to your right, through a wood and past a pond to a lane. Turn right and follow the road to Oxley's Green.

*G*o straight over the crossroads and follow the lane downhill. On reaching the sharp bend at the bottom, take the bridleway on your left, pass through the farmyard and turn left into the lane at the end. Turn right at the first junction, signposted to Burwash then, at the first house on the right, take the path opposite and follow this through a gate into Park Wood. When you reach a main gravel track, bear left then, near a small stream, bear right onto a path. Pass through a small gate on your left and cross two fields to a track near Park Farm. Turn right and follow to Bateman's, then turn right again and follow the lane to a stile on the left and cross to follow the path up to Burwash village car park.

Jack Fullers' (Free House)

Remotely situated, this cheerful pub has fine views of the Weald from its large garden. Within the mellow stone walls are two large adjoining rooms with old beams, huge fireplaces, oak tables, settles and kitchen chairs. Fresh flowers add a bright, homely touch. Children are very welcome, and highchairs are provided.

On draught: Brakspear PA, Harvey Best, Wadworth 6X, Heineken, Stella Artois. There is an impressive list of wines sold by the glass, and a range of English wines sold by the bottle. Food: Excellent pies include chicken and mushroom, prawn and halibut, gammon and onion, cheesy leek and potato, and cashew nut and aubergine – all at £4.25. Vegetable dishes (£1.10) are imaginative – honeyed carrots, cauliflower stilton, mixed curried vegetables. Traditional puddings are £2.25. Food is served at 12-2.30pm and 7-10.30pm, not Mondays (except Bank Holidays).
Telephone: (042482) 212.

The last folly can be reached from the pub by following the road to the left before resuming your circular route. Built in 1810, the 60ft Pyramid stands over Fuller's grave in the churchyard at Brightling, and it is said that he is seated inside, wearing a top hat and holding a bottle of claret.

Batemans (National Trust)
This magnificent house was built in 1634 for a local ironmaster, but is best known as the former home of Rudyard Kipling. It has changed little since the days when he wrote 'Puck of Pooks Hill', in which he describes the surrounding area. The study contains accoutrements of his day, and there is a working watermill in the garden. Kipling's splendid 1928 Rolls Royce can be seen in the garage.
Telephone: (0435) 882302.

East Hoathly *to* Chiddingly   Approximately 5 miles

*An easy, level walk
across pastures with
fine views towards the
South Downs.*

Parking
OS Map 199 Ref TQ5216. Car
park next to East Hoathly church.

Further Exploration
Chiddingly
There are magnificent views
from the churchyard over the
Weald towards the South
Downs and as far as Pevensey
Level. In the church, there is an
elaborate monument to Sir John
Jefferay, Queen Elizabeth I's
Chief Baron of the Exchequer
and further west are the remains
of his Tudor mansion,
Chiddingly Place.

*R*eturn to the main road, bearing left
into the village. At a sharp bend,
take the lane off to the right, passing the
King's Head, then turn right and follow the lane,
which turns into a track. In a short distance, cross a
lane and follow the footpath through a small wood.
Cross a stile and keep to the edge of the field, and
cross another stile on the left into a wooded area
before entering a field. Head straight for the gate
ahead, cross a lane, pass through another gate, and
keep to the visible path across grazing pasture through
gates towards the farm ahead. At the farm, pass
through a gate and follow the track to the quiet
country lane, bearing left to the picturesque village of
Chiddingly and you will soon see the pub on your
right.

*C*ross the lane towards the church and
take the waymarked path opposite
the village shop, behind some houses. Cross
the stile and follow the path across a field to a further
stile. Bear right, and head along the edge of the field
to another stile and continue downhill. Cross three
more stiles before reaching a narrow country lane,
bear right then, almost immediately, left across the
stile into another field. Head uphill along the
left-hand edge of the field, crossing a further two stiles
before passing through a gap in the hedge into an
arable field, again keeping to the left, and cross to a
stile visible in the hedge ahead. On the road, bear left,
pass Holdens Farm and then, around a right-hand
bend, take the driveway on the left. In a short
distance, bear right over a stile onto an arrowed path.
Cross the field to the edge of the hedge and continue,
keeping the hedge to the left, pass through a gate on
the left, then cross stile on the right and follow the
path beside a campsite. Cross a further stile and bear
right along the right-hand edge of the field. Walk
through woodland on a well-established path to a
road junction. Cross, and follow the quiet lane back
to the village and car park.

Six Bells (Free House)

 Behind the unassuming facade of this redbrick village pub lies a warm and welcoming establishment with a very individual character. Under the low beams are simple furnishings which include an antique settle box, Windsor armchairs, pews, old engravings, many prints and the occasional stuffed animal. The flagged floor is old and uneven and leads to a warm fire in the main bar. The back bar has a huge inglenook and there is a pianola with many rolls, which can be played with permission. Of particular note is the collection of old advertising signs out in the garden where there is plenty of seating, a rabbit hutch and a goldfish pond. Children are welcome in the small back room.

On draught: Courage Best and Directors, Harvey Best, Guinness, Hofmeister, Fosters, Kronenbourg 1664, Red Rock cider. Food: Bar food is tasty and excellent value for money. A changing blackboard menu includes French onion soup (60p), cheesy garlic bread (£1.15), beef and vegetable pie (£1.60), salads from (£1.70), and chilli con carne (£2.95). Puddings (£1.30) include treacle pie and banoffi pie. Food is served at 11-2.30pm and 6-10pm. Closed Mondays (except Bank Holidays). Telephone: (0825) 872227.

Henley *to* Lickfold

Approximately 8 miles

There are some steep parts in this Sussex walk. However, there are rewarding views and very few other walkers about. The area is so widely signposted that it is important to follow carefully the directions given here.

Parking

OS Map 197 Ref SU8925 on the road near the Duke of Cumberland pub.

Opposite the pub car park, by the telephone box, you will see a footpath signposted. Follow this for a short distance to another footpath sign on the left. Turn down this path which loops round and goes uphill again. Follow the footpath sign straight ahead to a junction, into the woods and then take another footpath up a steep hill. At the next track crossing, bear left down to another signpost. Here the track is steep downhill to a more marked track where you bear right. At a narrow lane, turn left, pass a house called Nightingales and continue down the hill. Shortly after the road bends to the left, follow the footpath to the right by the fir copse to the next signpost, where you turn left, downhill. As you get to the woods, take the right-hand path. Bear right past some houses to the main road. Turn left to a footpath sign on the right, through a hedge. Cross the stile here, continue alongside the hedge and follow the signpost to the next stile. Cross the field to the left-hand corner, then turn right and walk around the outside of the field. Cross the stile, turn left and follow the footpath straight ahead. Once through the iron gate, take the right of the two signposted footpaths in the corner of the field, cross the stile ahead and carry straight on to the pub.

Lickfold Inn

 This was originally a simple country pub which, within the last 15 years, has been given a large 'Tudor' extension. A blazing log fire and low beams make it very popular, and the gardens are large with plenty of seats for the summer. No children under 14 are allowed inside whatever the weather.

On draught: Fuller ESB, Adnams, Hall & Woodhouse Tanglefoot. Food: A large menu includes various ploughmans (from £2.50) to steak chasseur at (£8) and roasts, stews and pies. Telephone: (07985) 285.

*T*urn left out of the pub and left again up the lane. Pass Hoewyck Farm and, where the road bends to the right, follow the footpath straight ahead. Go through a galvanised gate into a field, keeping to left-hand side. Follow the footpath signs and stiles through the valley, along the path of telegraph wires. At a tarmac road, turn right and through a pair of gates you will see a footpath sign pointing through woods. Don't follow this, but continue for a short distance to a footpath sign pointing across a field on the left. Cross the stile and turn uphill across the field to a stile on the right. Cross this and follow the footpath. Cross the little bridge, and then another bridge leading uphill to a track. Turn right and follow this track which starts to go uphill. Shortly after this, you turn sharp left at the footpath sign. Walk up the grassy ride, and cross another. At a footpath sign, turn left uphill to a tarmac road by a house. Walk up to the road where you left your car.

Penshurst *to* Chiddingstone

Approximately 6 miles

A beautiful Wealden walk through peaceful meadows, woodland and parkland.

Parking
OS Ref TQ5243 Map 188
Penshurst village.

Further Exploration
Penshurst Place
Originally a medieval manor house, Penshurst was converted into a grand estate by the Sidney family in the 16th century, and has connections with Ben Johnson and Lady Pembroke, the sister of Sir Philip Sidney (author of *Arcadia*) who was born here in 1554. The chestnut-beamed great hall is the oldest and finest in the country, and the state rooms are furnished lavishly. There is a toy museum, Tudor-style gardens, an adventure playground, a countryside exhibition and a nature trail. Telephone: (0892) 870307.

Chiddingstone Castle (National Trust)
This 17th-century contains Stewart and Jacobite paintings, Egyptian and Oriental antiquities, and a collection of Japanese lacquer and swords. Telephone: (0892) 870347.

From the village centre, follow the B2176 north past Fir Tree Tea Rooms on the left and Penshurst Place the on right. In a short distance, take the lane on the left leading to Salmans Farm. Cross the River Eden and bear right onto a bridleway. Through a farmyard, turn right on the lane, soon to follow a waymarked footpath on the left into mixed woodland. Take the footpath on the right, signposted to Chiddingstone village, cross a stile, walk along the edge of a field, then diagonally across the field to another stile. Follow the path down to a quiet lane, bear left into Chiddingstone and the pub.

Return along the lane, bearing left, pass the oast house and Larkins Brewery, and follow the lane down to the bridge over the river. Cross, then cross a stile on the right and bear right across a field towards a small white footbridge. Follow the yellow arrows and paths across fields and through a gate onto a road. Bear right for a short distance, then take the waymarked path through a farm, keeping the farmhouse to the left. Cross a hop field and a meadow to a gate, and join a quiet lane beside a railway bridge. Bear right and follow the lane to a road junction. Turn left and almost immediately right, onto an arrowed footpath into woodland. Take the path to the right, and keep right at the next fork. Remain on this path to a stile, cross, bear right, then left down through woodland to another stile and enter the beautiful parkland of Penshurst Place, heading downhill through an avenue of oak trees. Two-thirds of the way down, bear right and head towards a stile. With the lake on the left, head towards a stile and black sign ahead, then straight towards the large house. Cross the drive and leave the parkland at the church. Through the churchyard, turn right on the road back to the village.

Castle Inn (Free House)

 Owned by the National Trust, the building dates from 1420, but became an inn in 1752. It is tile hung from roof to ground, with latticed windows overlooking the peaceful churchyard. Inside, the main bar has been modernised well, with settles around tables, sturdy cushioned wall-settles, oak beams and floor, and a fine open stone fireplace. The public bar is simpler, with wall-settles and a few chairs, and has a darts board, shove-ha'penny and dominoes. There is a separate restaurant and an enclosed garden with a small bridge across a pool and rockery to a lawn with sturdy picnic benches. Children are welcome in the eating area of the bar.

On draught: Larkins, King & Barnes Sussex, Shepherd Neame Master Brew, guest ales, Guinness, Carlsberg, Hurliman. Food: Good, appetising bar food includes sandwiches (from £2.50), ploughmans (£3.40), filled jacket potato (from £2.80), beef and Mackeson pie (£4.35), and salad (£6.55). Desserts include Dutch apple slice and cream (£1.85) and Amourette Cointreau (£1.95) Food is served at 11-2.30pm and 7-10.30pm. Telephone: (0892) 870247.

Lenham *to* Ringlestone

Approximately 6 miles

A challenging walk mainly through farmland, with a super pub at the halfway point.

Parking
OS Map 189 Ref TO9052
Lenham square.

*L*eave the square by the Faversham Road to join the main A20. Cross theroad, turn left and continue alongside it for a short distance before turning right into a field and striking diagonally to the left towards a black silo. At the junction of the Pilgrims' Way and a road, continue in the same direction across another field, keeping to the left of a small copse near a farm. At a paddock, head for a stile leading onto a road. Cross the road and follow the footpath opposite leading through a wood to reach a junction of tracks. Turn here down to an iron gate and again onto the road. Turn right, then right again through another iron gate set back from the road. Head towards a stile with a blue marker in the left-hand corner of a small copse, then towards a stile near some buildings, leading to a metalled road. Cross the stile immediately opposite, and follow the yellow marker to another stile into a static caravan site. Keep left and follow the path over three more stiles, and into the field. Continue straight up the hill and climb over the stile to the right of the pub.

Ringlestone Inn (Free House)

Built in 1533, this was originally a hospice for the monks travelling along the Pilgrim's Way. The original brickwork and beams are complemented by antique furniture, flagstone floors and some unusual additions, such as the small bread oven tucked away in the main room, and the 17th-century sideboard behind the bar. Outside, there are picnic tables on the raised lawn. Children are welcome.

On draught: There is not space enough here to list all of the beers offered, but they include Felinfoel Double Dragon, Archers Headbanger, Goacher's Maidstone Ale and 1066, Mitchells, Shepherd Neame Bishop's Finger and Spitfire, three stouts, six lagers, two ciders and 24 English fruit country wines. Food: The hot and cold buffet often includes sausage and onion plait, chicken and leeks in cider, loin cutlets in mushroom sauce (all around £3.65). Food is served at 12-2pm and 6.30-9.30pm. Telephone: (0622) 859900.

*T*urn left out of the pub and take a track to the left alongside a large house. Through an iron gate, bear right to a stile with a yellow marker. Cross, and continue over another stile into some woods. At a field, bear right to a gap in a hedge just before the pylons, then straight across to a road. Turn left to a T-junction, then right. Cross the stile alongside an iron gate and descend to another stile and, eventually, to a road. Follow the path opposite across a field to a junction of tracks. Take the wide, grassy track to the right. At a large oak tree, turn left and, keeping the hedge to your left, continue through a gap then cross the field diagonally to meet a grass track. Keeping the woods to your right, cross two fields, climb the hill and cross the stile to a road. Turn left, then left again at a fork. Just before you reach a cottage, follow the footpath to a small copse, which you skirt to the left before crossing a stile into the woods. Out of these woods, descend, keeping the wood to your left, to a road. Turn left then right, cross the A20, and take the Faversham road back to Lenham.

One Tree Hill *to* Stone Street

Approximately 6 miles.

A peaceful walk with magnificent views over the Weald of Kent.

Parking
OS Map 188 Ref TQ5553
National Trust car park.

Further Exploration

Ightham Mote (National Trust)
This medieval manor house has an attractive garden and a moat. Though extensively remodelled through the centuries, it is a fine example of medieval architecture. Of particular note are the Great Hall, the Old Chapel, and the Jacobean fireplace and frieze in the drawing room. Telephone: (0732) 810378.

Knole House (National Trust)
This is one of the largest houses in England, having been extended and refurbished by Henry VIII and ten generations of the Sackville family. The state rooms are rich in architectural detail, fine portraits and outstanding furniture. The 26 acres of grounds feature formal walks and a herd of deer. Telephone: (0732) 450608.

*L*eave the car park at the bottom right-hand corner through some staggered fencing, following a wide footpath to reach the top of an escarpment. Follow the path to the left, through an open area with a seat, and along the top of the ridge until you reach more staggered fencing and a National Trust sign indicating One Tree Hill. Through the fencing, at a T-junction, turn right and follow the well-trodden footpath through some woods. At a road, cross, and follow the bridlepath almost opposite. Follow the yellow footpath markers and bear left at a fork, which leads to a stile before another escarpment. Follow the trail down to join another path next to a wire fence. Turn left and continue over a stile, down some steps to pass a derelict cottage on your left. Cross a stile to the right of a metal gate, when the track is joined by another descending on the left. Continue straight on, through the farmyard of Mote Farm to a road, with Ightham Mote directly opposite. Turn left and continue uphill to find a track to the left, opposite a pretty cottage. Follow this past a stone building on your left, up through some woods, and through an orchard to a metalled road. Turn right to the pub.

Rose & Crown (Free House)

This busy little pub is thought to be 150 years old. The bar has a cheerful, rustic feel, with some exposed masonry, a collection of jugs hanging from the ceiling, and vases of flowers on the tables. The patio area has a number of picnic tables, and there is a secluded garden with shady trees.

On draught: Fremlins, Flowers, Whitbread, Heineken.
Food: The very varied menu will satisfy most palates, from fresh salmon maison (£3.75) to pasta of the day (£3.95), and filet steak au poivre (£8.95). Food is served at 11.30-2.30pm (Sunday 12-2pm) and 7-9.30pm. Telephone: (0734) 810233.

*R*eturn to the point where the footpath met the road and take the trail on the opposite side of the road, which leads diagonally to the left through the orchard – ignore the bridle path which goes straight ahead. At the end of the orchard, cross the road and take the public bridleway passing Lord Spring Farm Cottage on your right. The track becomes a sunken footpath through woods to reach an access road to two houses on your right. Continue on this road to a fork. Bear left through some woods, to a fenced path between some houses, leading to the road. Turn right until you meet a track crossing behind the playing field. Turn left past two cottages to reach an entrance gate to Knole Park. From here, go straight ahead, passing a pond on your left, until you meet a metalled road. Follow the track over the golf course, passing a keeper's cottage on your right, to find the exit from the park onto a road. Immediately opposite is a road signposted to Under River, which you follow to the end where the One Tree Hill car park will be found off to the right.

West Hanger *to* Shere

Approximately 5 miles

This walk takes in part of both the North Downs Way and the Pilgrims' Way, and is mainly a gentle walk with a steep climb at the end.

Parking

OS Map 187 Ref TQ0548 West Hanger car park

Further Exploration

St James's church, Shere
There is an interesting mixture of architectural styles in this building, which was originally constructed in the 13th century. Original features include the font of Purbeck marble and a large chest which was likely to have been used to collect money for crusades. There is also a medieval stained glass window which contrasts with the 20th-century restoration work by Louis Osman.

At the far side of the car park, turn right down the metalled road and continue down the hill. Where the road bends sharply to the right, take a footpath leading off to the left. Past the stables of Hollister Farm, go through a gate and keep along the path, over a junction with another footpath. At the next junction of footpaths, turn right, heading towards Gomshall. Along the ridge where there are views of the village to the right, take the footpath to the right which leads down to the A25 to the west of a petrol station. Cross the road and follow Queen Street, signposted to Peaslake. At the road junction, turn left down Gravel Pits Lane, then turn right by Gravelpits Farmhouse, and follow the footpath to a gate and across a field. At the far side of the field, bear right through a gate, heading towards Shere church, where you will find the pub.

White Horse (Watneys)

This rambling old inn has been a hostelry since the 17th century, although parts of the building date back to the 15th century. It is full of nooks and crannies, with old fireplaces, low beams and several small side rooms. Children are welcome in the eating area.

On draught: Ruddles Best and County, Webster Yorkshire. Food: There is a good range of bar meals, including sandwiches (from £1.50), ploughmans (from £1.95), stilton, leek and tomato pie (£3.95), and sirloin steak (£6.95). Food is served at 12-2pm and 7-9.30pm. Not Sunday evening). Telephone: (048641) 2518.

*T*urn right out of the pub and walk through the village. Just past the museum, turn right along Pilgrim's Way. At a group of houses, follow the path round to the right, then to the left. At this point, a small churchyard is seen to the left, while the path bears right to a gate. Go through the gate and follow the path to the left beside the Tillingbourne stream. On reaching a gate, go through it and turn right, crossing a ford on a small bridge. Pass a house on the left and then take the footpath on the left, and walk through the woods and over a stile into an open field. Walk across the middle of this field, to the elaborate Apostolic Church, built by Pugin around 1840. Turn right beside the road to meet the A25 and cross it carefully to the Silent Pool car park. Walk to the right side of the car park and follow signs for the Silent Pool. The path follows the left-hand side of the Silent Pool, the place where King John is supposed to have caused a peasant girl to drown by driving his horse at her. At the far end, climb a short flight of steps and follow the path into the woods. After a short distance, the path goes up the right-hand side of a field and into the woods. Near the top of the hill, you meet the North Downs Way, marked as a public bridleway. Turn right and follow the North Downs Way back to West Hanger car park.

Leith Hill *to* Abinger Common

Approximately 5½ miles

This is a predominantly woodland walk going through some traditional Surrey villages.

Parking

TQ1343 Leith Hill Car park (south) at Starveall Corner

Further Exploration

Leith Hill Tower is a remarkable viewpoint of 965 ft with views south towards the coast (which can be seen in fine weather). To the north are the skyscrapers of Central London. This is the highest point in southeast England.

Abinger Common

St James' Well in the far left corner of the grassy area, was put up in 1893 and has an ornate roof in addition to well-preserved winding gear. Just across the road is a large house – Goddards – designed by Edwin Lutyens and built in 1899.

Walk back to the road and turn left. A very short distance down the road is a path leading through woodland to Leith Hill Tower, to the rear of which you take the path heading north, into the woodland of Wotton Common. At the first fork, bear right and further on, bear left. At a clearing, follow the right fork. After about ¼ mile, this path leads into a clearing where there are three paths leading out. Keep left to a metalled road going to Broadmoor. Turn right, pass Leyland's farm on the left and take the footpath off to the left down the far side of the farm property to an old stile. Walk round the edge of the field to the right, to reach the footpath at the far side, threading to the left down an overgrown track. Just past the house on the right, cross the stile on the right and follow the path to an unmade road, past two cottages and some farm buildings, and down the hill to a T-junction at Abinger Bottom. Turn right, continue through the village, up a hill into the woods. A little way past the clearing on the right, a footpath leads off to the right at an angle. Follow this until it eventually meets a metalled road. Turn left, and the pub is on the right, opposite the church.

Abinger Hatch (Free House)

 In a peaceful village setting immediately opposite the church, this white-painted inn offers good food and refreshment. The large bar leads through to a spacious garden with bench seats. Children are welcome.

On draught: King and Barnes, Hall & Woodhouse Badger Best and Tanglefoot, Wadworth 6X, Ringwood Best, Toby. Food: A selection of light meals includes soup (£1.50), ploughmans (£2.50), filled jacket potatoes and basket meals (hot meals average around £4). Food is served at 12-2pm and 7-9pm. On Sunday afternoons, cream teas are served. Telephone: (0306) 730737.

Cross the road, the village green beyond and go over the stile into a wide field with the footpath crossing through the centre. At the far side is another stile and after this, the path enters the woodland of Abinger Common. Keep straight on until you reach a gate by a duckpond at Holmbury St Mary. Turn left onto the road, walk through the village, and take the road that leads off to the left, signposted to Abinger Common and Leith Hill. As it bears round to the left, take the footpath signposted to the right through Pasture Wood. After just over a mile, at a junction by High Ashes Farm, turn right and then right again at the next junction away from the road. Keep left at the next two junctions, and the path soon leads to two five-barred gates. Take the footpath to the left back to the road, and the car park is across the road to the left.

Box Hill *to* Mickleham   Approximately 6 miles

*An extremely hilly
walk with some chalk
slopes being
particularly steep and
slippery after rain – so
care should be taken.
The walk also gives a
vivid insight into the
devastation caused by
the recent hurricanes.*

Parking

OS Map 187 Ref TQ1751
National Trust car park, (£1 to
non members).

*F*rom the National Trust shop, cross the road into the car park and then the open space behind it. Go to the far left-hand corner of the green and follow the grey arrows, turning left along the indicated track. Follow these numbered marker posts into the woodland, beginning with number one. At the foot of some steps, by post eleven, turn left (ignore its arrow pointing right), to follow the chalky track, which descends along Juniper Bottom to reach a small car park, alongside a cottage and road. Cross the road and ascend the very steep, wooded chalk hill. At the top, keep round to the right with the main path, pass the seat in a clearing and head into the trees again. At the black, iron corner- post, turn left, then left again at another post and descend to a wide track. Cross, and pass through the squeeze gate in the wire fence opposite. Descend the narrow, footpath and cross the stile beside some white gates. Continue along the gravel drive and, at Mickleham church, take the second gate to the right into the churchyard. At the stone wall, keep along the footpath beside the gardener's shed, past a large house, then across a track. On the nearside of a cottage, turn right along another path. Pass a school, and, shortly on meeting a road, turn right again up to the pub.

King William IV (Free House)

Cut into the hillside above the main A24, this narrow, unpretentious little pub is extremely popular during the summer months. Its attractive paved patios and grass seating areas provide plenty of tables on different levels, with varying degrees of intimacy, and there is also an attractive wooden shelter looking down the hill. Inside, the two snug bars are homely and welcoming, with a nice chatty atmosphere. Children are welcome in the front bar.

On draught: Adnams, Wadworth 6X, Hall & Woodhouse Badger Best, Heineken. Food: The menu includes pasta with carbonara sauce, salad and French bread (£3.95), Chinese-style chicken on rice (£4.95), steak, kidney and mushroom pie cooked in Guinness (£3.95), filled jacket potatoes (from £2.95), and ploughmans (from £2.95). Food is served at 12 – 2pm (booking advisable for large parties). Telephone: (0372) 372590.

*T*ake the narrow footpath up the far side of the pub, ascending steeply by steps at first. Shortly, cross to the small path opposite, and continue up to the top. Turn right onto a wide track (much tree clearing work taking place here), and follow this round to the left. At a fork, keep to the left, then keep straight at the next two junctions. At the third junction, turn right then keep left as the track opens out from between the trees onto White Hill, to follow a wide, grassy track. In about ½ mile , pass the NT signpost for Mickleham Downs, then turn right down another track on the nearside of a fence, eventually to reach the road below. Turn right then, in about a mile, turn left back into the Whitehill car park. Return to the grey marker post eleven. Keep ahead here, to follow the grey waymarked nature trail posts once again. Continue to the top of the hill at post fifteen, where paths cross, and turn right with the grey arrow. Continue ahead with all subsequent markers through the trees to the open green. Cross back over the green and return through the NT car park to the shop.

Further Exploration

Box Hill

One of the most popular viewpoints in southern England for over 200 years, Box Hill, at 564 ft, is a designated Country Park. At its summit, beside the car park, there is a National Trust shop and information centre (open Wed-Sun, afternoons only), toilets, snack bar and restaurant. A number of waymarked walks radiate from the Centre, where there are leaflets on sale. From the summit viewpoint near the main car park, there are magnificent views towards the South Downs, while in winter, its steep north facing slopes are popular with tobogganists.

Maidensgrove Scrubs *to* Upper Maidensgrove

Approximately 4½ miles

A quiet, undulating walk through beech woods and across farmland with pleasant Chiltern views.

Parking

OS Map 175 Ref SU7287
Warburg Nature Reserve car park

Turn left out of the car park, then right past Pages Farm and follow the arrowed track through beech woods until you reach a house and a junction of tracks. Turn right on to the path signposted to Russell's Water and walk past a new house on the left, through a gate, and across a field to a stile on the right. Follow the white arrows across two fields to another stile and a junction of paths. Go straight ahead (orange marker with green arrow) along the established track. Emerging from a small beech copse, cross the stile on the right (arrowed) and continue uphill. Cross three stiles on the left at top of the field before crossing another field and reaching a quiet lane. Turn right and you will soon reach the pub.

Five Horseshoes (Brakspears)

This very popular country pub is set high up on a common among beech woods, with fine views across the Chilterns from the peaceful, large garden. It is a beautiful, creeper-clad cottage of brick and flint whose two neat, comfortable bars have large inglenook fireplaces, low ceilings, wheelback chairs around wooden tables, and some cushioned wall-settles. The lounge bar walls and ceiling display an impressive collection of banknotes from all over the world. Children under 14 are not allowed in the bar.

On draught: Pale Ale, Special, Guinness, Heineken, Stella Artois. Food: The large menu includes Stilton soup (£2.25), smoked chicken pancake (£4.75), ploughmans (from £2.95), and seafood lasagne (£6.25). Puddings include creme brûlée and banoffi pie (£1.95). Food is served at 12-2pm (12-1.30pm Sunday) and 7-10pm (7-9.30pm Monday, Friday and Saturday). No bar food Sunday evening. Telephone: (0491) 641282.

*T*urn left out of the pub and follow the quiet lane into Russell's Water. Passing the pond, bear right along the track near the Beehive pub and follow the sign to Pishill With and Stonor. Pass round the back of Upper Nuttall Farm, following the arrowed path through the edge of the wood. At a junction of paths, bear right and continue around the edge of the field to a wood. Follow the white arrows on trees through beech woods and scrubland, then cross the stile at the top of the hill and pass between two fenced paddocks towards Maidensgrove Farm. Cross the driveway to a gate and a track beside Maidensgrove Common. Cross the lane to an arrowed footpath through Maidensgrove. At end of the hamlet, near a farm, take the footpath on the right next to the Wiltshire Cycleway sign. Cross the stile and follow the footpath downhill through woodland and part of Warburg Nature Reserve, back to Pages Farm, with the car park on the right.

Nuffield *to* Stoke Row　　Approximately 5¾ miles

An easy walk through a mixture of wood and arable land on established tracks, with pleasant views across rolling landscape of the southern Chilterns.

Parking

OS Map 175 Ref SU6687. Grass verge outside Nuffield Church.

Further Exploration

Maharajah's Well is in the village of Stoke Row. This incongruous Indian well was a 19th-century gift to drought-stricken Stoke Row from the Maharajah of Benares, who had befriended an Englishman from the area. The well is 300ft deep, 4ft wide and is covered with an ornate, Indian-style cover.

*F*rom the church, which is the highest point in the southern Chilterns, walk left along the lane and take the Ridgeway path off to the left. Cross a stile and continue straight on, through a narrow stretch of woodland, following white plastic labels with orange arrows. Pass Upper House Farm, bearing left on joining its driveway. Follow the track, keeping left, and cross a small country lane, soon passing in front of Oakingham House on the right. Keep to the well-established footpath across gently rolling arable land, enter the woodland and join a road. Turn right, then take the next footpath on the right into the woods. Pass through two gates, crossing a field to an opening in a hedge, soon emerging in the pub's extensive back garden.

*R*eturn through the garden and wood to the lane and bear right, shortly turning left to follow a waymarked path up through woodland. Join a gravel track and follow uphill to Newnham Hill Farm, bearing left at a small pond and passing in front of another house, into a farmyard. Keep directly ahead, through two gates, and cross a field parallel to a hedge. At a wood, cross a stile, and bear right onto the footpath, to an established track, where you turn left. This track will take you through the wood, and then through arable land, passing behind Howberrywood House and on through more quiet arable and partly wooded countryside. Where the track leaves the narrow strip of woodland at the first sharp bend, ignore the stile to the left and take the footpath into the wood a little further on the left. Follow the path through woodland and, on reaching a cottage and driveway, bear left and take the narrow path beside the fence and house. Turn left into the lane, then right back to the church.

Crooked Billet (Brakspears)

This friendly 17th-century pub oozes character and epitomises all that a true country pub should be. The main building has two bars, both with large fireplaces, an array of sturdy tables and chairs, and a collection of bottles, mainly champagne, adorning every visible ledge. There is no bar as such, just a hatchway, and good quality ale is fetched from the cellar straight from the barrel. A brick extension offers a lounge with armchairs, a settee and more comfortable chairs and tables. Walls are hung with a variety of prints of local scenes. The three acres of garden have a few picnic tables and lots of room for children to run around.

On draught: Pale Ale, Special, Old Ale, Heineken, Stella Artois. Food: There is an wide selection of imaginative home-cooked meals specialising in unusual fish dishes. The menu includes freshly dressed Cromer crab with Dijon mayonnaise (£3.95), Guinea fowl, red wine and bacon (£6.95), and fricassee of chicken, bacon and mushrooms with gnocchi (£6.95). Desserts include chocolate refrigerator cake (£2.50), blackcurrant pie and custard (£1.95), and grilled goats cheese, garlic, salad and bacon (£3.95). Food is served at 12-2pm and 7-10pm (booking advisable). Telephone: (0491) 681048.

Ayot St Peter *to*
Ayot St Lawrence

Approximately 5½ miles

Parking

OS Map 166 Ref TL1916
Outside the church of Ayot St Peter.

Further Exploration

Shaw's Corner
This was the home of George Bernard Shaw from 1906 until his death in 1950. There are many literary and personal relics in the downstairs rooms, which remain as in his lifetime.
Telephone: (0438) 820307.

*T*ake the path directly opposite the church, and follow this, bearing right at the fork, between woods and a field, until you reach a gate at the road. Turn left at the edge of the field, not onto the road, and aim down to the bottom corner and some woods. At a fork, bear right and then, at a road, turn right again. At a bend in the road, follow the farm track on the left, heading towards Linces Farm. Before you reach the farm, take the signposted footpath to the left, following it downhill through fields, aiming for a gap in the trees straight ahead. This part of the walk is not very well-defined, but it is a public footpath. Go through this gap, turn left and walk along the side of the field, keeping straight and heading uphill as far as a hedge. Turn left here, head towards Ryefield Farm, and follow the tarmac drive to the road, where you turn left. After almost ¼ mile, turn right on to a bridleway which seems to cross over the road. (There is a post, but it has lost its sign). Keep straight through the fields, on towards some buildings and a road. Turn right and signs will point you to Shaw's Corner, but before you reach it, you will see the pub on your left.

Brocket Arms (Free House)

There is a very cheerful atmosphere in this pub. Walkers are welcome, and there is a lobby in which you can leave muddy boots and other walking gear. Inside the pub, there are old beams and brasses, while outside there is plenty of seating in the pretty gardens. Children are welcome.

On draught: Greene King Abbot and IPA, Wadworth 6X, Adnams Bitter, Harp, Heineken, Kronenbourg 1664. Food: A la carte meals are available in the separate dining room, but usual bar meals include a cold buffet (from £2.50). Food is served at 12-2pm and 7.30-9pm. Telephone: (0438) 820250.

*T*urn left out of the pub, past an old ruined church to a junction – Shaw's Corner. You will see a footpath on the right and one on the left between two fields. Follow the latter to the end of the field where there is a small footpath bearing right into some woods. If the bridleway is slippery, it is a good idea to follow this through the wood and then out onto the bridleway again, heading downhill to a road. Cross the road, bearing slightly left, and the bridleway continues through more fields and woods straight to a bridge. Climb the steps to the right-hand side of the bridge and turn left to go over the bridge, following the disused railway line as far as the road. Turn left here and you will soon be back at your car.

Whiteleaf *to* Little Hampden

Approximately 6½ miles

A peaceful walk amongst the beech woods and vales of the northern Chiltern hills.

Parking

OS Map 175 Ref SP8203 Whiteleaf Cross picnic area.

Further Exploration

Chequers can be seen in the distance on your outward journey. Built in 1580, this fine old house was restored by Lord Lee of Fareham, who gave it to the nation in 1919 as a country residence for the Prime Minister. Its name is said to derive from a 12th-century landowner who was a clerk of the exchequer.

*F*ollow the Ridgeway path from the car park (acorn and blue arrow) along the edge of the Chiltern ridge until you reach a grassy clearing on the ridge edge. Follow the path marked with a yellow arrow on the right down through beautiful beech woods, following white arrows on trees. Cross a stile and follow the path to a quiet lane. Cross, then turn right onto an arrowed track up the valley. At the first junction of three paths, follow the narrow path ahead uphill into mature beech woods and look for directional white arrows. Continue straight on, ignoring other paths, until eventually, you reach a gate opposite a farmhouse. Bear right onto a wide track and follow down to a road across open farmland. Cross this road and follow the arrowed path around the farmhouse uphill into some woods. The path takes you through the woods, then to the edge of an arable field, where you cross a stile and keep to the path through more woodland down to a quiet lane, and the pub on the right.

Rising Sun (Free House)

Tucked away up a quiet lane amongst beech woods, this is a popular haunt for walkers – although muddy boots and dogs must be left outside. An unassuming, redbrick building, it has tables on a small terrace at the front. Inside, there are three small bars with comfortable chairs, bench seating, stripped wood panelling and floral curtains. Very popular for food, its main emphasis is towards a smart dining pub. Children are not allowed after 8pm.

On draught: Adnams, Hall & Woodhouse Tanglefoot, Marston Pedigree, Greene King IPA, Beamish, Hacker-Pschorr. Food: Good, imaginative food includes daily specials such as Tandoori chicken with cucumber raita and garlic bread (£4). Food is served at 12-2pm and 7-9pm. Closed Sunday evenings and all day Monday. Telephone: (0494) 488393.

*B*ear right out of the pub and soon take the waymarked path on the right beside a house. Cross a field and walk down through a wood on an established path. At the end of the wood, bear left around the edge of the wood, passing near some horse jumps. Cross the field to a hedge, bear right down to a road, cross, and over the next field you will reach another road. Signs will direct you across the stile, and over the road into Hampden estate parkland. Bear diagonally left uphill across the field towards a gatehouse. There, turn right along the driveway towards the church. Keep straight on through the grounds, with the house on your right and barns to your left. Pass through a gate and keep straight along the edge of a field, eventually entering woodland. Keep following the white arrows on the trees, then go straight on at a track. After walking along the edge of a field to the left, you will reach a track and stable where you bear right onto an arrowed path through more woodland. In a short distance, take the first path on the left through beech woods and join the outward route near the ridge. Bear left back to the car park.

Stonor *to* Turville

Approximately 6 miles

A very peaceful amble through mixed woods and across open fields and parkland, with beautiful views over rolling Chiltern countryside. The woodland is a haven for woodpeckers, squirrels, finches and titmice.

Parking

OS Map 175 Ref SU7388
Extensive verge area on B480, entering village from the south.

Further Exploration

Stonor House and Park
Home of Lord and Lady Camays, the house dates back to 1180. It has a medieval Catholic chapel and some of the earliest domestic architecture in the county. The building's treasures include rare furniture, paintings sculptures and tapestries. The house is set in beautiful gardens and has a delightful deer park. Telephone: (049163) 587.

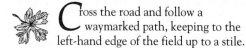

Cross the road and follow a waymarked path, keeping to the left-hand edge of the field up to a stile. Cross and follow white arrows painted on trees uphill through glorious beech woods bordering a private estate. Joining a track, bear left and pass through Coxlease Farm, keeping the farm buildings to the right. At a junction of tracks, keep left to join a quiet country lane, turn left and follow the lane as far as Kimble Farm. You will soon see the waymarked bridleway. Follow this as it turns into an established track through unspoilt countryside, before entering extensive mixed woodland and reaching a quiet lane. Bear right, cross a stile and follow the waymarked path on the left across a field. Keep to marked paths down into the village of Turville, and you will soon find the pub on the right.

Turn left out of the pub, past the church and the cottages. On entering woodland, take the footpath on the right, passing a woodman's saw and log store, and continue along the field edge up to a stile. Cross and walk uphill along a narrow path into beech woodland and turn right on the main bridleway at the top. At a junction of bridleways, turn left towards Turville Court and join a lane. In a short distance, cross a stile and take the waymarked path downhill to a lane. Cross two stiles and a large field to another stile at the top of the rise. Over the next field and another stile, bear right onto a concrete driveway, join the road and turn left. In a short distance, bear right onto a waymarked footpath into woodland, and follow the white arrow markers down through coniferous forest. Pass through a gate into Stonor Park, keeping to the marked path, then join a road, turn left and walk through Stonor back to the car.

Bull and Butcher (Brakspears)

Tucked away in the heart of this beautiful village within a fine Chilterns Vale, this is a small black and white cottage close to the small green, church and a few picturesque cottages. Typical of the village local, it has a two-room bar with low ceilings, open fireplaces, and cushioned wall-settles around sturdy wooden tables. There is a freshness about this pub, with flowers on each table, and a stable door half open in warm weather. Walls are adorned with local prints and photographs, and shelves contain numerous plates. There are fruit trees in the very pretty garden where barbecues are held on summer Sundays. Well-behaved children are allowed in the eating area.

On draught: Pale Ale, Special, Old Ale, Guinness, Stella Artois. Food: Excellent food is all homemade and ranges from substantial meals to light lunch snacks. A changing blackboard menu includes Somerset pork (£5.25), various ploughmans (£2.95), port, Stilton and walnut pate (£3.50), Brakspear pie (£4.95) and salads (from £4.25). Puddings include walnut pie or chocolate bombe. Food is served at 12-2pm and 7.30-10pm. Telephone: (049163) 283.

Bucklebury Common
to Frilsham

Approximately 6 miles

A peaceful, low-level ramble through thick forests and across open farmland.

Parking

OS Map 175 Ref SU5569
Bucklebury Common car park.

*T*ake the track away from the road to join the main gravel track across this part of the common, shortly crossing a lane. Keep to this track and turn right at the first junction of paths. On joining another track, bear right, passing a house on the left, and keep straight on as the path narrows through the woods. The path soon becomes less visible as forest clearing has been carried out, but keep between the coniferous trees and the cleared section, and you will soon pick up the established path which eventually leads to a quiet lane. Bear left into Bucklebury. Pass through the churchyard and take the footpath across the field to another lane. Follow this, bearing left at the junction. Gently climb uphill before taking the waymarked path on the right (near a farm), across a field to a further stile and between more fields. Follow the yellow arrows to the dense woodland and continue on the established path through the trees, up some steps, eventually bearing left on joining a wide track. At a quiet lane, turn right and follow this for ¼ mile to the pub.

Pot Kiln (Free House)

A gem of a true rural pub, this small brick cottage is in an unspoilt location overlooking large fields of cows and thick woodland. Inside, there are three bars leading off a small lobby. The bars are attractive and unspoilt, simply furnished with benches and pews, wooden floors and open fires. The lounge bar has numerous prints on the walls, while the smaller public bar has old pub games available, such as dominoes, shove ha'penny and cribbage. Children are welcome in one of the bars.

On draught: Arkell BBB, Morland Best and Old Speckled Hen, Murphy's, guest beers. Food: An interesting range of good home-prepared bar food includes filled rolls (from 80p), ploughmans (£2.50), beef goulash (£3.95), chicken pie and salad (£4), country lentil crumble and salad (£3.95), macaroni cheese and granary roll (£2.95). Food is served at 12-1.45pm and 7-10pm (rolls only on Sunday). Telephone: (0635) 201366.

*B*ear left along the lane and take the waymarked path on the right, across a field and stile into woodland. Keep on this path (blue arrows) across a junction of paths, and continue through tranquil woodland. When the path descends towards a house on the left, look for a narrow path on the left through trees (if you arrive at a driveway, you have gone too far). Pass around the back of the garden and along the edge of woodland, and head towards a stile. Cross, and bear to the left of a house, soon following yellow arrows and joining a driveway. Follow this to a lane, cross and continue to a small brook. Cross the wooden bridge and keep to the path across arable land, straight on at a fingerpost. Cross a stile and head uphill across a field to the right of a house. Cross a stile, bear left down a lane, then take the waymarked path on your right into woodland, eventually arriving at a house with pigeon lofts. Bear right, then left, and keep left before joining the main track across Bucklebury Common. Turn right and follow the track back to the car park.

Hungerford *to* Kintbury   Approximately 5 miles

A pleasant and easy walk through the lovely Kennet Valley; the first half is along the towpath of the Kennet and Avon canal, the return across farm and common land.

Parking

OS Map 174 Ref SU3468. On the town edge of Hungerford Common, by the cattle grid and the Down Gate pub.

Further exploration

Hungerford
This is a very attractive old town with a wide main street and lots of antiques and other interesting shops – a pleasant place to browse around.

Elcot
A little way north of Kintbury, on the other side of the A4, the gardens of the Elcot Park Resort Hotel are open to the public throughout the year, free of charge. This is also a major hot-air ballooning centre and the skies around here are often full of balloons of all shapes, sizes and colours.

*T*ake the road which leads off the common and into the town centre. At the end, turn right into the high street, pass under the railway bridge and at the canal bridge, take the footpath on the right to reach the towpath. Turn right and follow this until you reach Kintbury, crossing to the other side of the canal at the first road bridge. The canal, the river Kennet and the main line from Paddington to the west, run parallel here, with the old Bath Road (A4) close by. At Kintbury, cross the road bridge by the station to the pub.

Dundas Arms (Free House)

Dundas is the family name of the local nobility, the Earls of Craven. The pub which bears their name is charming and unspoilt and has a lovely situation bordered by the canal on two sides. On a fine day, it is worth arriving early to get a table beside the water – you may also see passengers boarding the colourful narrow boat opposite the pub for its afternoon trip to Newbury. Inside the pub, there is one good-size bar with old dark wood furniture, and prints and china on the walls. There is also a separate restaurant which has a very good reputation. Well-behaved children are allowed into the bar, but no dogs are allowed while food is being served.

On draught: Morland Ordinary and Old Speckled Hen, Adnams Boys, Eldridge Pope Hardy County, Guinness, lagers. Food: Excellent home-cooked bar meals include crab au gratin (£3.50), Gravadlax (£5.90), steak and kidney pie (£5.50), fresh pasta (£4), smoked salmon quiche with salad (£4), sandwiches (from £1.50), and ploughmans (£3.80). If you still have room, try the chocolate brandy cake or bread and butter pudding. Food is served at 12-2pm and in the restaurant only in the evenings. Telephone: (0488) 58263.

*T*urn left out of the car park, cross the bridge and follow the road through the village of Kintbury. Take care on the section without pavement, it is quite busy and very narrow. At the end of the village, fork left towards Templeton and Inglewood Health Hydro. Continue along this delightful country lane, passing through two pairs of impressive gateways; the second marks the entrance to Inglewood Health Hydro, where the rich and famous retreat to be pampered. Ignore the bridleway opposite, the footpath you need is a little farther along on the right and is clearly signposted. Take the path straight across the field to a little wooden bridge over a drainage ditch. Here you need to keep straight, but follow the edge of the field a short way to the right. Beside a small group of trees, the path continues between two hedges, eventually bending round to the right. Do not turn with the path, but keep straight along the edge of the next field. At the end, cross a farm track and continue along the edge of the next field. At the far end, cross the stile onto Hungerford Common. Keep straight across the common until you reach the intersection of the common roads. Follow the road to the left – you will see the edge of Hungerford at the far end – and this will bring you back to the cattle grid and the Down Gate pub.

Great Bedwyn
To the west of Hungerford, this village has a small but fascinating museum of stones, explaining the secrets of the stonemason's craft and the language of the carvings.

Further west again are the Crofton Beam Engines, one of which is the oldest working steam engine in the world (1812). For details of steam weekends, telephone: (0672) 870300. Narrow boat trips are also available here – telephone: 081-290 0031.

Streatley *to* Aldworth   Approximately 6½ miles

A gentle walk with splendid views of the Thames Valley and open downland.

Parking

OS Map 174 Ref SU5980 Streatley High Street, or try verges along unclassified road off the A417, or the railway station.

Further Exploration

Aldworth Church (take the lane down from the pub past the old-fashioned Post Office shop) is famous for its remarkable monuments of the de la Beche family. There are nine effigies, thought to date from the 14th century, and they are so large that they are locally called the Aldworth Giants.

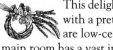 Walk up the main street and turn right at the crossroads. Where the road forks, take the left-hand A417 Wantage road and follow this lane, skirting the ridge of the Downs. The path leads past Thurle Grange and Thurle Grange Farm to Warren Farm, where the Ridgeway becomes a bridlepath leading quite steeply uphill to your right. After a short uphill stretch, ahead on your right you will see a short stretch of woodland, Ham Wood. Past the edge of this, take the well-defined farm track leading off almost at a right-angle on your left, going downhill, then briefly uphill, to join Ambury Lane. Turn left into the lane and walk down into Aldworth. Where the road forks, keep left for the pub.

Bell (Free House)

This delightful inn is a long, low building with a pretty garden to one side. The bars are low-ceilinged and beamed, and the main room has a vast inglenook fireplace. Mementoes of the village cricket team adorn the walls.

On draught: Hall & Woodhouse Badger Best, Morrells Mild, Arkell BBB and Kingsdown. Food: Bar snacks consist of a wide range of filled rolls which are excellent quality and value (from 70p to £1.30). Food is served at 11-3pm and 6-11pm. Closed Mondays. Telephone: (0635) 578272.

Turn left out of the pub and follow the lane to a T-junction with the B4009. Turn left and follow the road through Hungerford Green to Westridge Green, pass a manor house on your right, then take the footpath to the left beside a farm. The path leads through level farmland, then steeply downhill through woods to emerge into an open downland valley, crossing the bottom of a field with steeply sloping sides. At the edge of the field you meet a band of trees and join a track on your left leading back to the Ridgeway lane at Thurle Grange Farm. Turn right for Streatley, or left if you have parked on the lane nearer to Warren Farm.

Approximately 5 miles   # Oxford *to* Godstow

*T*ake the A420 westwards out of the town, and pass the railway station on your right. At the river bridge, turn right onto the path on the nearside bank and follow the river north. Cross the Oxford Canal by bridge and continue along the riverbank. The next small bridge carries the path onto Fiddler's Island, at the end of which, cross the river to the opposite bank and Bossoms Boatyard. Continue along this bank to Binsey. From here, there are wide expanses of grass by the river, popular with picnicking families and paddling children – it was along this stretch of river that Lewis Carroll first told the story of Alice in Wonderland to the young Alice Liddell. Pass through the gates at Godstow Lock, and you will have the extensive ruins of Godstow Nunnery on your left. Pass through the gate and turn right to cross the ancient bridge to the pub.

The return walk simply retraces your steps back the way you came.

This is a very easy walk, with a well defined and level path following the banks of the river.

Parking

Oxford town centre, or 'Park and Ride' on the edge of the town. Roadside parking difficult near to start of the walk as it is mainly for resident permit holders. Parking at the railway station costs £5 for non-rail users. The walk begins at OS Map 156 Ref SP5006. Those arriving by train can join the walk immediately outside the station.

Trout Inn (Free House)

Dating from the 12th century, this lovely old inn, originally the guest house for the nearby Benedictine nunnery, has certainly adapted well to today's trade. The whole river bank outside the inn has been provided with seating for summer drinks, and peacocks and bantams roam between the tables. Inside, the inn retains its ancient character. Children are allowed inside, as are well-behaved dogs if kept on a lead.

On draught: Bass, Greene King IPA, Guinness, Tennents, Carling Black Label, Dry Blackthorn cider. Food: There is a separate counter serving lunches in the summer and a regular menu on offer in the main bar, including chilli, curry, a wide choice of both salads and ploughmans, at prices ranging from £2.50 to £6. Food is served at 12-2.30pm and only in the restaurant in the evenings. Telephone: (0865) 54485.

Sandford St Martin *to* Great Tew

Approximately 6½ miles

A delightful walk through undulating North Oxfordshire countryside and through idyllic honey-coloured stone villages.

Parking
OS Map 164 Ref SP4226
Sandford St Martin church.

*H*ead north out of the village and in ¼ mile, take a track off to the right (by a yellow hydrant) towards some thatched cottages. Pass in front of the cottages and follow the path through a gate and across the field, keeping to the wall on the left. Pass through a gate and follow the path beside some houses onto a lane. Bear left to the crossroads where you keep straight until you reach a turning on the right leading to Hobbshole Farm. Pass behind the farm and bear left onto a track, keeping to the left-hand edge of the fields. You will eventually follow the wall of Great Tew Park on the left before passing through two gates, and following a lane past some beautiful thatched cottages, into the village, with the pub immediately to the right.

*B*ear right in front of the row of honey-stoned thatched cottages, and cross the small green on the left beside the school, passing through a kissing gate over the quiet lane. Bear diagonally left uphill across a field and pass behind the farm. Through a gate, cross a field, keeping to the right-hand edge, to a stile and a road. Cross the next field diagonally, keeping the radio-mast to the left. At the corner of the field, join a lane and bear right into Little Tew. Take the waymarked path beside the first house on the left, cross a stile and head for another stile in the hedge. Bear diagonally right across the field towards a farm and join a road. Turn right and, in a short distance, cross a small brook and turn left along the track beside it. Pass through a gate towards a derelict house, soon bearing right through another gate. Keep to the footpath along the right-hand edge of the field and eventually join a lane near Tracy Farm. Turn left and follow this lane, keeping left towards woodland, then turn right towards Beaconsfield Farm. On nearing the farm, take the track on the right and follow this to the lane, where you turn right back to Sandford St Martin church.

Falkland Arms (Free House)

 A feeling of timelessness prevails in this Grade 1 listed, partly thatched, wisteria-covered building. Inside the honey-stoned building, the bar has a superb inglenook fireplace, stone-flagged floors, high-backed settles, oak panels and beams, and a ceiling bedecked with a collection of old beer and cider mugs. The bar is tiny, but claims to disperse more different traditional ales in a year than any other pub in Britain. You can also buy clay pipes and tobacco and many different kinds of snuff at the bar. Outside, there is a front terrace with tables and chairs, and a garden at the back with more seating amongst the geese and ducks. Children are welcome in the eating area.

On draught: Donnington Best, Hook Norton Best, Wadworth 6X, Theakston XB, Ringwood Old Thumper, Beamish, Tuborg, and regularly changing guest ales. Food: Traditional bar food is wholesome and served in generous portions. A changing blackboard menu includes lamb stew (£4.50), vegetable lasagne (£4), faggots (£4) and ploughmans (from £1.50). Food is served at 12-2pm (not Sunday). Closed Monday lunchtime. Telephone: (060883) 653.

Witney (Mills) *to* Minster Lovell

Approximately 5½ miles

This is not an arduous walk; it takes you through the fields and water meadows near the River Windrush west of Oxford to the Cotswold stone village of Minster Lovell. Look out for the tiny 9cm Goldcrest which, with the Firecrest, is the smallest European bird.

Parking

OS Map 164 Ref SP3510. Just outside Witney on the A4095, Burford Road, there is a long lay-by for free parking.

Next to 18 Burford Road, opposite Moor Avenue, is a track marked 'No entry for unauthorised vehicles' and a 15 mph sign. This start of your walk is somewhat uninspiring but keep going and you will soon be in the fields alongside the river. Follow the track round to the left through a 5-barred metal gate into the fields with the River Windrush to your right. Cross the next stile and continue until you see New Mill to your right. Cross the next stile and turn left up the side of a field. Cross the main road, following the yellow arrows marked with CW (circular walk). Cross the field and over another stile into some woods. Keep following the yellow arrows until you see the river opens up to a pool where there is a wooden bridge. Make for the churchyard ahead and follow the grassy track through it where, beyond the gravestones and to the left of the field, you will see a metal gate. Pass through this and the playing field, towards yet another metal gate, and there you will see the pub.

Old Swan (Hall's & West)

This is an attractive 600-year-old building of warm Cotswold stone with a flagstone entrance hall. On your way to the neat and simple bar, you go through a room which has open log fires crackling at either end. Outside there is a large garden with tables, benches and a pool with a fountain. Service is attentive and prompt.

On draught: Morland Original, Wychwood (local brew), Kaltenberg, Strongbow cider. Food: A wide range of sandwiches is available, from ham (£1.95) to the great steak sandwich (£4.20), and little extras such as a tasty dill sauce which comes with a smoked salmon open sandwich. Homemade soups and Oxfordshire bangers and mash (£3.95), as well as other hot dishes, are on the menu, plus several desserts, all at about £2 each. Food is served at 12-2.30pm and 7-9.30pm (booking advisable for the restaurant in the evening). The pub is also open for afternoon teas (set tea £3.75 per person). Telephone: (0993) 774441.

Further Exploration

Minster Lovell Hall and Dovecot
The ruins of this 15th-century house are steeped in history and legend. Among its many former inhabitants, was Francis Lovell, an important and powerful supporter of Richard III, who made him a Viscount in 1483. It has been claimed that Lovell's skeleton was found seated at a table in the celler of the hall in 1728. Also of interest is the medieval dovecot which has survived intact through the centuries. Telephone: (0993) 75315.

*T*urn left out of the pub, up the hill and after the last house on the right-hand side of the road, there is a stile over which you climb and aim towards the factory chimney at Crawley. Walk on towards the rising ground, to a track lined with hedgerows, past some houses and down to the main road. Turn right and then first left up the hill. Take the track on the right for Field Farm ('Beware of the Bull' signs need not worry you; this is a public right of way and anyway, bulls do not roam around freely). At the end of the track, to the left and obscured somewhat by farm clutter, is a stile over which you climb and follow the narrow path down to a field, turn left, cross it and find the gateway and track that leads past the side of New Mill. Cross the small wooden bridge ahead and walk along the side of the river to your left, through a gap in the fence. By now you will recognise the field from which you started earlier and you can rejoin the track back up to the road to your car.

Chedworth *to* Withington

Approximately 6½ miles

A peaceful walk through Chedworth Woods, with their Roman remains, and along the River Coln. Lookout for deer, pheasant, woodpeckers and numerous types of trees within the wood - larch, spruce, old oak.

Parking

OS Map 163 Ref SP0512 Near Chedworth church.

Further Exploration

Chedworth

This is a large scattered village on the steep hillsides bounding the Coln valley. Fine old cottages radiate from the church which has Norman origins and a medieval manor house. Above the village at Denfurlong, a farm trail provides insight into modern dairy and arable farming. Open all year.

*F*ollow the lane to a gate and stile and cross the field, heading towards a house on the hill. Bear left away from the house to cross a stile into a wood. Go uphill, cross a stile and keep straight on along the right-hand edge of the field, eventually crossing another stile into Chedworth Woods. Follow the main path, waymarked 'Roman Villa', and take some steps on the left to join the old railway line. Turn right and follow this along a deep cutting. Just before the path reaches private property, bear right up a bank to a quiet lane. Turn right and follow the lane down to a waymarked path on the left. Cross a stile, bear diagonally left down to Coln Valley, pass through a gate and follow the yellow arrows across the river and uphill to join a path running parallel to the river. Pass behind a house to join a track, bear right and join a lane. Turn right for a short distance before taking the waymarked path on the left near a house, eventually passing in front of the Mill House, across the drive to the road and the pub.

Mill Inn (Samuel Smith)

Delightfully situated beside the River Coln with a lovely garden, this 500-year-old pub was built to accommodate workers from the nearby mill whose original site is now an island in the garden, connected by a small bridge. The main rambling bar is full of nooks and crannies, and has little side rooms in which children are welcome. There is an attractive bay window seat with good views of the neatly kept gardens and the local duck colony.

On draught: Samuel Smith Old Brewery, Museum Ale and Extra Stout, Ayingerbrau, Prinz. Food: The standard bar menu includes ploughmans (£2.95), basket meals (from £2.50), steak and mushroom pie (£4.50) and steaks (£8). Puddings include Mississippi mud pie, Death by chocolate, and treacle and walnut tart (all £1.40). Food is served at 12-2pm and 7-10pm. Telephone: (0242) 89204.

Chedworth Roman Villa (National Trust)
Sheltered in a beautiful combe, the villa is the best exposed Roman-British villa in Britain. Built in about AD120, it was occupied until AD400. Mosaic floors are fine examples of a craft practised some 1,500 years ago. Fascinating finds and plans of the site are displayed in the adjacent museum. Telephone: (024289) 256.

*F*ollow the lane right uphill and turn left at the next junction. Pass a large manor house and bear left at the next junction, soon taking a waymarked path across stiles and diagonally left across fields down to Withington Woods. Follow yellow arrows and red markers on trees. At a major fork in the path, follow the yellow arrow to the left, turn right at a junction, and follow the red dot down to the main track. Turn right, then right again and follow the path through a clearing, past a pheasant enclosure, and then bear off right, following arrows. At a T-junction, bear left and follow the path to a road. Cross this and a stile, and follow the left-hand edge of the field, over another stile into a small stretch of wood, before bearing right (red dots on posts) on a path towards an old airfield. Bear left along the old runway to a road, turn right then, at a junction, bear left, remaining on the lane into Chedworth. Bear left at the next junction, then left, and left again along the drive to Manor farm. Where the drive swings round to the left, cross the stile on the right and head downhill, cross the stile into the churchyard, and return to the car.

Wootton-under-Edge *to* Waterley Bottom

Approximately 6 miles

Not for the faint-hearted, this is quite a strenuous walk, especially the first part which is is not well signposted. For the less ambitious, there is an alternative outward route. The views are superb, especially from the viewpoint at North Nibley which overlooks the Severn Estuary.

Parking

OS Map 162 Ref ST7593. Outside a converted church (now used as auction rooms) just off the B4060.

*T*ake the footpath to the right of the church down the hill through a cul-de-sac and up the other side. Cross the lane and, after a short distance, turn right and take the path up to the top of Coombe Hill. Turn left along a track, then left again and, at the next junction, bear right before crossing a stile onto the road and turning right. (For an easier walk follow the road sign to Waterley Bottom – there is little traffic and the lanes are narrow.) After the driveway to The Ridings on your left, just before the lane joins the main road, take the second footpath on your left. Cross the field to the far hedge and turn right uphill keeping the hedge on your left. Over the next stile, follow the contours of the hill. At the opposite hedge, head for a stile in the corner of the field, keeping the hedge on your left. Cross the stile and turn left across two fields towards the woodland. Through a gate into the wood, turn right at the bottom of the slope. Take the main track, which has a bar across it, then turn left. Keeping left, follow the arrow over a stile into a field, down to the valley bottom and up the steep slope to the next wood. Turn left at the top and, at the next fork, turn right uphill. Take the next left and turn left into the lane. After about a mile, turn right to Dursley, and right again to the pub.

the new inn

New Inn (Free House)

This isolated pub has two bars and a very well kept garden, for which it has won many prizes. Many of the beers are served from a collection of antique beer engines. Dogs are allowed in the garden only.

On draught: Cotleigh WB and Tawny, Smiles Best and Exhibition, Theakston Old Peculiar, Greene King Abbot Ale, Castlemaine 4X, Lowenbrau, Guinness and guest beers. Food: The standard menu offers large helpings of ploughmans (from £2.10), pasties (from £1.80), chicken and mushroom pie (£2.95), with desserts such as peach and banana crumble (£1). Food is served at 12-2pm and 7.30-9.30pm. Telephone: (0453) 543659.

*T*urn right outside the pub at the junction, then take the next right. Follow the lane for about a mile and, at the next junction by a pillar box, turn left. Just before the next junction, take the footpath on your left alongside a house, up the hill and through the woodland. At the top, turn right up the slope into the trees. At the next junction, turn right downhill. Take the steps up the side of the gully on your left, to the monument built in 1886 in memory of William Tyndale, first translator of the Bible into English. Follow the path alongside the wire fence on your right, and the path from now on is well signposted. Follow the path to the right. At the next junction, take the right fork, then the next left. Come out of the wood and take the middle track into open fields. The path comes down to a promontory with a copse of trees encircled by a wall, first planted to commemorate the victory of Waterloo. Take the path to the left and turn right down the slope to a tarmac path. Turn left after crossing a stile then, after a short distance, turn right down Old London Road. At the bottom, turn left on to the B4060. Walk down Gloucester St to the junction, then left to the old church where you left your car.

Stanton *to* Snowshill   Approximately 6½ miles

This is a classic walk along the Cotswolds ridge with panoramic views across the Vale of Evesham, taking in three of the most picturesque golden-stone villages.

Parking

OS Map 150 Ref SP0634. Car park on edge of Stanton village.

Turn left onto a lane and enter the charming stone village of Stanton, bearing left at the first junction into the main street lined with honey-coloured stone houses. Walk up the main street to a small green, and bear right along a lane which soon becomes a footpath – the Cotswold Way. Follow the yellow arrows uphill through a gate onto a track. The climb uphill is quite long, but rewarding. At the top, pass through a gate near a farm and cross the field to bear right along a track through the farmyard and around the front of the house. Bear left to a gateway, turn left, then right diagonally across two fields on an established path. On reaching a track, turn right and continue into Snowshill. The pub lies opposite the church and village green.

Snowshill Arms (Donnington)

This attractive stone pub is beautifully situated next to the village green which is enclosed by charming period cottages. Inside, the airy open-plan beamed bar is partly panelled, with stripped stone walls visible in places. Simple furnishings include comfortable wall-benches, pine tables and seats on a carpeted floor. Some prints and local photographs adorn the walls. Good seating is available in the garden which has a play area for children, and valley views.

On draught: Donnington Best and SBA, Guinness, Lowenbrau, Carlsberg. Food: Basic bar food includes sandwiches (from £1.25), ploughmans (£2.25) and steaks (£6.25). Food is served at 12-1.40pm and from 6.30pm onwards. Telephone: (0386) 852653.

*R*etrace your steps along the lane until you reach Oat Hill farmhouse, where you take the waymarked path downhill through a gate. Follow yellow arrows and posts on the footpath across fields towards a farmhouse on a hill. When you join a track, bear left, then right onto a track which goes round the back of the farm. Follow this to a gateway, where you bear left across the field towards an old stone gatepost. Cross the nearby stile and follow the arrowed path downhill. On reaching a stile at the bottom of hill near Buckland Manor, bear left and follow the yellow arrows across fields to Bredon Hill and to the wooded hillside – Shenbarrow Hill. Past the north of Laverton village, Stanton soon comes into view. Take the arrowed path down towards the church and continue alongside the wall into the churchyard and eventually onto Stanton's main street. Bear right, then right at the end, back to the car park.

Further Exploration

Stanton is the perfect Cotswold village, totally unspoilt, with its main street lined with beautiful golden-stoned houses with steeply-pitched gables, most dating from 1600. Tucked behind the village cross is St Michael's Church which is particularly notable for its furnishings by Sir Ninian Comper. Some medieval pews survive, their poppy heads gouged deep from the days when shepherds took their dogs to church and fastened them to the pew heads.

Snowshill Manor (National Trust)
This 16th-century manor house has a terraced garden full of old-fashioned roses, shrubs and ponds. Inside is the collection amassed by Charles Wade, including English, European and Oriental furniture, craft tools, toys, clocks, bicycles and musical instruments. There is also a collection of Japanese Samurai armour. Telephone: (0386) 852410.

Moreton-in-Marsh *to* Blockley

Approximately 5 miles

A gentle walk in open countryside which encompasses Batsford Park and Aboretum.

Parking

OS Map 150 Ref SP2032 Town centre car park, except Tuesdays.

Further exploration

The church at Blockley is well worth a visit. It was founded in 855 AD with most of the building dating from 1180 AD, with changes being made over the years until as late as 1929.

Batsford Arboretum

The 50 acres of land contain one of the largest collections of tree in Great Britain, and there are many rare and beautiful species. Telephone: (0608) 50722 and (0386) 700409 (weekends).

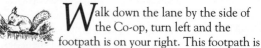

Walk down the lane by the side of the Co-op, turn left and the footpath is on your right. This footpath is well signposted with arrows by the Cotswold Warden Service. After a short distance, take the gate into an open field and follow the track across the field for nearly a mile, until you reach a copse on the right. Turn right here over a stone bridge, and follow the path alongside the copse for nearly ½ mile. Ignore all turnings and stiles off the path until you reach a stone wall with a signpost. Turn right over the stile and the path will lead you along the south-east boundary of Batsford Park to a road. Turn left and walk along the road up the hill, past the turning to Batsford. At the next junction, continue straight up the steepest part of the hill, along the road. At the top of the hill, take the signed footpath into a field straight ahead and follow this path for about ½ mile. At the junction of several paths, follow the blue arrows downhill and take the left fork. At the road, turn right, slightly uphill, then take the next left. This will lead you to the pub on your right.

Crown Inn (Free House)

This golden-stone Elizabethan inn is situated in the heart of the village. The bar has a mixture of antique and smart new furniture, and the cosy lounge has Windsor chairs, traditional cast iron-framed tables and an attractive window seat. There are two bars, and two restaurants. There are also tables set out on the main street and in the old coach yard. The staff are friendly and dogs, but not children, are allowed in the bar.

On draught: Wadworth 6X, Everards, Courage Directors, Fosters, Kronenbourg 1664, Guinness, Beamish, guest beers. The wine list is excellent and very extensive. Food: The fish restaurant has fresh fish delivered three times a week from Cornwall, and offers dishes from peppered mackerel (£2.95) to whole Dover sole (£13.95). Daily specials include pork fillet and thyme sauce (£6.95), and avocado and stilton bake (£3.95). There are also usual sandwiches (from £1.60) and ploughmans (from £3.75). Food is served at 12-2.15pm and 7-10pm in the bars and fish restaurant (7-9.30pm in the a la carte restaurant). Telephone: (0386) 700245.

*O*ut of the pub, turn right then take the next left down a steep hill. At the end of the lane, turn right up a hill. At the next junction, turn left and cross the road. The signposted footpath is on your right, and leads across open fields up the hill past a farm house, to a stile. Cross, turn left through the trees, go through the next gate and turn right following the stone wall on your right. Cross the road into the wood and follow the stone wall on your left. Cross the trial course and follow the path to a track. Turn right down this track and, at the next junction, bear left. The path then goes across open fields and the main drive to Batsford, and back to the path into Moreton-in-Marsh. You rejoin it at the junction alongside a high stone wall, with Batsford Park on your left. Retrace your route back to the village.

Cotswold Falconry Centre
Situated by the Batsford Arboretum, daily demonstration of the art of falconry can be seen here. Telephone: (0386) 701043.

Sezincote
For a taste of the exotic, visit the Indian-style house which was the inspiration for the Brighton Pavilion. There is also a charming water garden in the beautiful grounds.

Lower Slaughter
to Naunton

Approximately 7½ miles

A beautiful walk across open Wold landscape, along the Windrush and Eye Valleys and through three much adored Cotswold villages.

Parking

OS Map 163 Ref GR1622. Village road opposite Manor Hotel.

Further Exploration

Lower Slaughter and Upper Slaughter

These two small villages sit a mile apart along the River Eye, and are rich in honey-coloured stone houses dating from the 16th and 17th centuries. Lower Slaughter has numerous bridges across the Eye and a charming row of cottages near the 19th century corn mill, the only brick building in the village. Upper Slaughter stands on a grassy hill above Slaughter Beck, once dominated by a Norman castle whose remains of a motte and bailey can be seen. An outstanding Elizabethan manor house with 15 tall chimneys and an avenue of tall trees, dominates the village, which was once the home of diarist Francis Witts, whose mortuary chapel is in the church.

*F*ollow the River Eye upstream through the village beside quaint rows of stone houses. Turn left at a small traffic island and follow the peaceful lane to a T-junction. Go straight along the established waymarked bridleway, cross a road, through two gates and follow the path across a field towards the tranquil Windrush Valley. Bear left onto a wide bridleway, through a strip of woodland, and bear right along the path to cross the River Windrush beside the elegant Mill House. Climb the drive and bear right at a T-junction, following blue arrows through Aston Farm, across a field and into mixed woodland. Continue through the woodland along a quiet but muddy path above the river. At a gate, continue straight before the path drops down to follow the river upstream. Cross stiles and fields to a road near Lower Harford Farm, cross the road and keep to the arrowed path. At a gate cross the small bridge and head uphill over a stile, then left through a gate and, descend, through gates, over a tiny bridge and into Naunton. The pub lies on the right, down the lane.

Black Horse (Donnington)

This is an unpretentious pub with a flagstone floor, beams and simply furnished with country-kitchen chairs and built-in oak pews, with stripped stonework and a huge wood-burning stove in the main bar. The lounge, with its open fire, is a snug retreat. The pub offers a number of games such as cribbage, dominoes and shove-ha'penny. Outside there are a few tables with views down the lane. Children are not allowed inside.

On draught: Donnington Best and SBA, Guinness, Lowenbrau, Carlsberg. Food: Plain, popular bar snacks start with home-made soup (£1.25), chicken liver pâté (£2), marinated herring fillet (£2.50), ploughman's (from £2.25), half roast duck (£8), and beef casserole (£4.50). Puddings include chocolate truffito or lemon brûlée (£2). Food is served 12-1.30pm and 6.30-9.30pm (Sunday from 7pm). Telephone: (0451) 850378.

Turn right out of the pub, then right again up the lane and take the waymarked path on the right across a field to a gate. Follow the blue arrows across fields and alongside a wall to a road. Take the bridleway beside the wall, running parallel to the road, and cross the road on reaching a gate. Follow the track through two gates near a barn and cross a field. Pass through three more gates and head down into the valley, bearing left onto a road near a row of cottages. At a post-box on the right, take the bridleway beside the river. Gradually climb to a gate by a house and keep to the waymarked path towards the river. Join the bridleway to the village, bear left over the stone bridge and follow the path to a lane. Turn right, then left down the arrowed path, crossing a small stone bridge and two fields, and at fork in path, take the path diagonally to your right across another field to a kissing gate. Follow the path alongside the river and enter Lower Slaughter, bearing left towards the shop and mill, and take the riverside path back to your car.

Hidcote Manor *to* Ilmington

Approximately 5 miles

This walk has some steep slopes but is otherwise fairly gentle. Allow time at the end of the walk to visit Hidcote Gardens.

Parking

Left hand car park at Hidcote Manor.

Further Exploration

The church at Ilmington is worth a visit. It has examples of early Norman arches, and an early Norman bell tower. In Tudor times, the church was altered considerably with the addition of the first storey and the transepts. Above the south door is a medieval niche which would have held a statuette of the patron saint of the church.

Hidcote Manor Garden
These formal and informal gardens, laid out by Major Lawrence Johnston over forty years, contain many rare trees, shrubs and plants of all kinds. Open April - October. Telephone: (0386) 438333.

Walk through the gate at the end of the overflow car park (waymarked by yellow arrows). Walk diagonally across the field to your right, up towards the hedge, over the stile and over the next one immediately to the left, as signposted. Follow the path downhill and over the next stile. Through the wood to the right, cross the field diagonally to the hedge and stream. Over the stile, follow the path, keeping the hedge and stream to your left, across several fields, under a line of pylons to a road. Turn right to a T-junction, then turn right, and right again after Larkstoke Cottage. Take the next left, then before reaching the farmhouse, turn left into a field. Walk round the edge of the field to your right, over the next stile and cross the stream, soon crossing back and turning right up the hill, following the blue arrows. Over the next stile, follow the yellow arrows, keeping the hedge to the right. Soon after the top of the hill, turn right over a stile and follow the path across the field, keeping the pond on your left. Turn left before the third stile, follow the fence, go through a gate and follow the track between two houses (private drive sign). Turn left and, at the junction, turn right and then left. Follow this lane past the Red Lion, around the next bend, to your destination.

Howard Arms (Flowers)

Attractively situated overlooking the village green, this pub is neatly furnished with cushioned chairs, old-fashioned settles and comfortable window seats. There are heavy beams, a huge inglenook fireplace, and rugs covering the flagstone floor. Outside, there is a large garden, and picnic tables on the terrace. There is a separate restaurant. No children under 5 are allowed, and dogs must remain in the garden.

On draught: Flower's Original and IPA, Guinness, Heineken, Stella, Bulmer's Traditional cider. Food: The bar menu includes soup of the day (£1.50), sandwiches (from £2.45), ploughmans (from £2.85), homemade broccoli bake (£3.25), chicken liver and Cognac pate (£2.75), and swordfish steak (£6.25). Desserts include banoffi pie and chocolate rum torte (both £1.75). Food is served from 11.45-2pm (12-1.30 Sunday) and 6.45- 9pm (No food Sunday night). The restaurant is open from 6.45-9pm, Tuesday - Saturday, booking advised. Telephone:(060882) 226.

*T*urn right and walk past the village shop, alongside the stream, and turn right towards the church. Follow the path to the left out of the churchyard to the main street. Turn right, then left (signed as a dead end) and follow the lane round to the left, up the slope, turning right at the top. Bear right at the fork, cross into the gully and over the next stile. Turn left uphill, keeping the hedge and fence on your left. Turn right along the ridge and follow the bridleway as indicated by the blue arrows. Cross the road, pass through the gate, and walk diagonally up the field to your left. Through the trees, follow the path to your right alongside a stone wall. Cross over the next lane and follow the track down to Hidcote and the car park.

Little Drewchurch
to Carey

Approximately 7½ miles

A long, undulating walk across the quiet, attractive farmland of the Wye Valley.

Parking
OS Map 149 SO5231 Little Drewchurch church.

Walk through the village, pass the school and then turn right at the crossroads. At the top of the ascent, turn left towards Carey. In a short distance, turn left along a farm track, indicated by a footpath sign. Shortly after passing a group of cottages, turn right over a stile. Head diagonally across this large field towards the telegraph poles. At the stile, cross into an orchard, and over the next stile. Pass between some farm outbuildings to another stile beside a lane. Turn right, then beside an old cottage, turn left over a stile, take the footbridge over a stream, and continue, keeping an old tree line to your left. At the end of the trees, cross the next stile then, at the edge of a farm cottage, walk diagonally to the right, crossing an old orchard and following the footpath sign. Cross the stile in the left-hand corner and continue along the edge of a field. After the next two stiles, descend to the left above and behind a farm. Through the gate at the bottom, turn right, pass in front of the farm and continue down to the pub at Carey.

Cottage of Content
(Free House)

 This delightful, 500 year-old pub enjoys an idyllic, tranquil setting beside an old humpback bridge, and its cosy, beamed bars have open fires, flagstones and polished oak tables. Children are allowed in away from the bar.

On draught: Hook Norton Best, Old Hookey, Worthington Best, Marston Pedigree, Guinness, Carlsberg, Tennent's Pilsner, Stowford Press Traditional cider. Food: Food is wholesome and well presented, and the menu includes deep-fried Camembert with cranberry sauce (£2.50), Japanese chicken (£3.95) and baked trout filled with celery and walnuts (£4.50). Sweets range from chocolate fudge cake to Jamaica raisin ice cream (£1.50). Food is served at 12-2pm and 7-9.30pm (Friday and Saturday till 10pm). Telephone: (0432) 840242.

*T*urn left out of the pub and in about ½ mile, cross an old railway bridge. Beside an oak tree, turn right through a gateway and turn right at the end of a tree-lined avenue. Cross the stile, and the field, heading towards the bridge. Continue along the banks of the river, crossing all stiles, for about a mile. Leave the fields by the final stile to join a road. Pass Brae Cottage and, opposite the stile and footpath sign, bear right up a narrow road. Keep right at a fork, pass 'Stoney-ways House', and bear left to pass through a group of farm buildings and reach a main road. Turn right and in a short distance, turn left through a gateway onto the public bridleway which eventually leads to a narrow road. Turn right, keep straight at the fork and follow the next track on the right (footpath sign), shortly passing a stone cottage and through a gate. Follow the line of a small brook, then after passing beneath some minor power cables, head up the incline to a gate, turn left, pass through another gate before turning left over the brook, then right, keeping the brook to your right. Over the next stile, turn left up to another stile and a narrow road. Turn right for your car.

Clehonger *to* Ruckstall　　Approximately 5½ miles

A pleasant walk above the Wye Valley close to the cathedral city of Hereford. There are spectacular views over the river from the delightful Ancient Camp Inn, once the site of an Iron Age camp.

Parking
OS Map 149 Ref SO4637 Clehonger church.

*F*rom the front of the church, turn left and follow the road to a farm track on the left (footpath sign). Follow this past the farm and a group of cottages then, in a short distance, turn right. Follow the minor power line to cross the stile, and continue to a gate alongside a farm. Through this, turn left onto a minor road. When you reach an orchard on the left, turn right through a gateway (footpath sign). Across the field, bear left through a gate into a small copse. Descend through another gate alongside a cottage, past Tuck Mill and across a small brook before turning right through another gate. Keep left around the wire perimeter fence of a sub-power station, continue straight then, in a short distance, cross a stile, ascend the steps on your left, continue along the path to the pub.

Ancient Camp Inn (Free House)

This secluded inn derives its name from the Iron Age hill fort on whose ramparts it stands, some eighty feet above the Wye, offering breathtaking views along the river. Flagstone floors, open fires and wooden furniture characterise a rustic charm, while the lounge bar offers inviting sofas. Smart, casual dress is requested, but there is a very pretty front terrace on which walkers can enjoy a wonderful lunch and a stunning view. Well-behaved children are welcome at lunchtime only.

On draught: Flower's Original, Wood Parish Bitter, West Country PA, Guinness, Heineken, Stella Artois and Strongbow cider. Food: The imaginative menu here includes ham and celery au gratin (£4.75), Greek shepherd's pie with salad (£4.95), and cannelloni filled with Ricotta cheese and spinach (both £4.95), and ploughman's (£2.75). Sweets (£1.95) include iced coffee soufflé and hazelnut torte. Food is served at 12-2pm and 7-9.30pm. Closed Mondays, no bar food Sunday evenings. Telephone: (0981) 250449.

*L*eave the pub along its access road and car park, and turn right with the footpath sign. Descend the path and cross an open field to the river bank. Over the stile in the left-hand corner, cross a footbridge and continue along the river bank. At a junction of paths, turn left then pass through a gate and continue up a track to pass a cottage, then turn left over a stile to cross a field. Keep on this path over stiles, fields and a footbridge, heading for the distant Eaton Bishop church. At a road, turn left to Eaton Bishop, past the church then, at the telephone box, turn left on the nearside of a black and white cottage, and follow the signs through and across fields and two stiles, then take the left-hand fork to join the road. Just before you reach a tiny hamlet, follow the sign to the right across the field, alongside a wooded brook. At the end of the field, cross the stile and footbridge, then keep straight ahead to cross the next field on the side of a hill, away from the brook. Through the next gate, turn left and cross the brook by footbridge. Walk diagonally to the right towards an old oak tree, but staying at the foot of the hill. Cross another footbridge, then ascend the path past a small building. Cross a stile concealed in a shrub at the top of the hill, turn right to the end of the field, and over another two stiles to the main road. Turn left, then at the top of an ascent, turn left along a driveway, (footpath sign). At the far corner of the right-hand warehouse (where the road surface ends), turn right through the gate. Cross two more fields and stiles and return to the church.

Sollers Hope *to* Woolhope

Approximately 4½ miles

An extremely pleasant walk in quiet, wooded country high above the Wye Valley, following the line of Ridge Hill (758ft) and Marcle Hill, affording stunning views, back through soft, green farmland on the return to the tranquil Sollers Hope.

Parking

OS Map 149 SO6133 Sollers Hope church. Space is limited, so be careful not to block the farm entrance.

*H*ead east away from the front gate of the churchyard, cross the road and the stile opposite. Pass some farm outbuildings to the left, keep a small stream on the right then pass through a gate, cross the field and through a further two gates until, alongside an old stone barn, turn right onto a narrow road. At the top, turn left along another lane then cross a stream, and keep left up a track to begin the long ascent of a wooded footpath. At the summit, turn left over a stile (walkers sign) and climb the steps to cross a stile and continue along Ridge Hill, following the yellow footpath arrow. Cross the next stile to pass a triangulation pillar (758ft), then cross three more stiles before, in the corner of the field, descending the steps to a road which follows Marcle Hill. Opposite Hooper's Oak Cottage, turn left and descend a footpath. Through the gate, cross a large field, following the line of the hedgerow. Over the stile in the far right-hand corner, ascend through a small copse, climb the stile at the end, cross a field, and pass through the gate to join a wooded track. Descend this track, and later the tarmac road, to reach the pub.

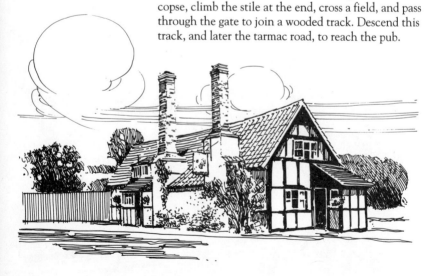

Butchers Arms
(Free House)

This is a distinctive black and white, half-timbered country inn, dating back as far as the 14th century. Welcoming log fires in winter warm its two cosy, beamed bars, while in summer, French windows open out onto a pleasant patio garden and stream. Children are welcome.

On draught: Hook Norton Best and Old Hookey, Marston Pedigree, Carlsberg. Food: Meals are well presented, tasty and homemade, and include ploughman's (£2.25), Woolhope pie, packed with rabbit and bacon and cooked in local cider (£4.25), mushroom Biryani and basmati rice cooked with spices and mushrooms, garnished with cucumber, tomatoes and coconut, and served with dhal (£4.25). Sweets are wonderful and extraordinary value at £1.25. See if you can finish the apple and almond strudel served with cream or the spicy prune and apple crumble with ice cream. Food is served at 11.30-2.15pm (Sundays 12-2pm) and 7-10pm (Fridays and Saturdays till 10.30pm). Telephone: (0432) 860281.

*T*urn left out of the pub to join the main road, and continue ascending gradually into Woolhope village. Pass the church and the Crown Inn and, in a short distance, turn left over a stile. Cross fields, stiles and a footbridge over a stream, keep to the right of the willow tree and continue over more stiles, a road and two fields to a farm road. Continue straight until you reach a fork in the path. Go through the centre gate (painted blue), and keep to the right-hand hedgerow. In the corner, climb the stile, follow the path round to the left, and cross the next stile up ahead over the stream. Keep straight along the right-hand hedgerow for a short distance, then cross another stile on the right. Walk along the right-hand fence line, through the gate in the far corner of the field, and continue, with a stream to your right. Through the next two gates, return through the farmyard to the church.

Bredwardine *to* Dorstone　　Approximately 7½ miles

An extremely hilly walk, predominantly on minor roads close to the Welsh border climbing to around 950 feet at its highest point, and negotiating some quite severe gradients (1 in 4 in places). But there are some wonderfully rewarding views over the Wye and Golden Valleys to distant Welsh hills.

Parking

OS Map 148 Ref SO3444
Bredwardine church

Further Exploration

Arthur's Stone

These stones are the remains of a chambered tomb of the late Neolithic period, dating from between 2000 and 3000 BC. A great slab set on upright stones was its entrance, probably used for burials of members of a family or community for several hundred years.

From the front of the church, bear right, around the outside of the churchyard. Through the gate, keep right to follow the path across the top of the old castle earthworks. Following the track downhill, pass through a gate and skirt a small lake. Pass through a gap in the hedgerow and cross a stone bridge over a stream, then keep to the right over a small hillock to a gate and a stile. Go through the gate and continue through another to the main road. Turn right to join the road (B4352) for a short distance before turning left to follow the Dorstone signpost onto an unclassified road. Begin the long ascent of Dorstone Hill and, after a mile, turn right to follow another road, signposted to Arthur's Stone, and continue to the summit. Turn left through a gate at the side of the stones (green footpath sign), to begin the long descent towards Dorstone through fields and gates, keeping the hedgerow to your right. Go left through the third gate and continue downhill, this time keeping the hedgerow to the left. Cross the garden of a new house by the two gates in its left-hand corner, and continue down a track and through the final gate. At the crossroads alongside Crossways House on the right, keep to the main road (B4348), ignoring the sign to the Pandy Inn. Go through the gate into Dorstone churchyard and follow the path round the church and out again. Cross a stream, pass a telephone box and keep on to the pub.

Pandy Inn (Free House)

The past still lingers on in this old, whitewashed pub set behind the green. And, in a history dating back over 500 years, Oliver Cromwell is listed amongst its former guests. Inside, beamed ceilings, worn flagstones, stout timbers, a vast open fireplace, and a somewhat rambling layout, envelop today's visitor in an atmosphere of rustic charm, and even now, one can conjure up images of England's one-time Lord Protector and leader of the Parliamentary forces, partaking the ale. Outside, there is a neat side garden for those wishing to dine 'al fresco', or for those who just need to air their weary feet after the climb. Chidren are welcome.

On draught: Bass Draught and Special, Allbright, Red Stripe, Carling Black Label, Guinness, Stowford Press Traditional cider. Food: Meals are wholesome and offer value for money. The changing blackboard menu might include smoked salmon mousse (£2.95), hummus with pitta bread and salad (£2.25), deep fried vegetables with dip (£2.95), pan fried trout (£5.95), cheese and broccoli pie (£4.50), steak and ale pie (£4.95), and ploughmans (£2.95). Sweets (£1.50) could include apple and cherry pie, treacle and nut tart, and chocolate fudge cake. Food is served at 12-2pm and 7-9pm (except Monday and Tuesday evenings in winter). Telephone: (0981) 550273.

For a magnificent view over the surrounding countryside, take a detour after about ½ mile on the unclassified road back to Bredwardine, the road bears round to the right. Go straight ahead here, over the stile beside a house, and the footpath leads on for 3\4 mile to Merbach Hill (1,043 feet).

*R*eturn to the crossroads beside Crossways House on your left. Here, turn left along a lane (No Through Road), cross a cattle grid and continue up a farm road. Turn right through the farmyard, ascending the farm track, shortly to cross another cattle grid. Continue with this track until you reach a further cattle grid, then turn right up a road. Ascend to the T-junction and turn left. This road descends very steeply to eventually reach Bredwardine village. Over the crossroads beside the war memorial and Red Lion Hotel, turn right along the tree-lined avenue back to the church.

Knucklas *to* Llanfairwaterdine

Approximately 5½ miles

This walk takes you along the river valley, on ancient tracks through pasture and woodland plus some bare windswept hillsides. There is a long steep climb on the returning journey.

Parking

OS map 137 Ref SO2574. Space may be found close to the village stores, otherwise head for the main road and a couple of spaces may be found at the end of the lane to Monaughty Poeth.

Walk towards Monaughty Poeth, over the River Teme and turn left towards Llanfairwaterdine. In just over ¼ mile, on a slight bend, turn right and go through an inset metal gate, up the valley keeping right of the fence. Climb the barbed wire (the path is definitely here although the way has been obstructed) and turn right onto a cart track towards a cluster of buildings and three tall pine trees. Through the gate, pass in front of a tumbledown cottage, then immediately turn left and cross a concrete farmyard into a paddock and old overgrown orchard, following the distinctive track alongside a hedge of nut trees until you reach a road. Turn left then, at a T-junction, turn right onto a rough track, soon turning left onto another old track. At the end of the wood, continue to follow the line of this ancient path into the valley and over a small brook to turn left up to the road. Turn left onto the road then at junction, turn right and pass the post office and its old GR post box, to the pub.

Red Lion (Free House)

Believed to be almost 400 years old this is a delightful traditional pub with a lounge bar complete with inglenook fireplace and a brick floored tap room with darts and skittles. Children are allowed only in the beer garden. No dogs.

On draught: Marston Pedigree, John Smith Yorkshire, Ansells Pale Mild, Skol, Strongbow cider. Food: A wide range of bar meals includes chilli, chicken (both £3.75), scampi and plaice and chips (£2.95). In the evenings, given a little more notice, more elaborate dinners are available, such as baked ham, chicken madras, and beef in garlic and red wine. Food is served at 12-1.30pm (except Tuesday when the pub is closed during the day) and 7-9.159m (not Sunday). Telephone: (0547) 528214.

Further Exploration

The small border towns of Knighton, Leintwardine and Clun are all in easy reach for exploration and so is Offa's Dyke, if more serious walking is required.

*T*urn left out of the pub, passing the village church, and in about ¼ mile, climb over a gate on your left, down to the River Teme and over the footbridge. Turn left, over the next gate and walk diagonally across the field to the right where you will see a gate in front of Goytre Farm. Cross the road and pass through a black gate up to the farmyard, crossing to another gate from which you now climb the well-defined footpath up the very steep hillside. At the top of the hill, keep going straight and you will quickly descend a good track to the valley. Near the bottom of the hill, bear right and continue around a hairpin bend to pass under a railway bridge. As you reach the farm buildings of Lower Hall Farm, turn left, passing in front of a diesel tank, and pass through the gate into the fields, keeping well to the left of Heyop Church. After about three fields, keep close to the railway embankment and you will find a stile that allows you to cross the railway – it is a well-used railway track so do beware of trains. Climb over the next stile and immediately turn right onto the road and continue to the village stores and your car.

Pant *to* Llanyblodwel

Approximately 9 miles

There is considerable climbing involved in this route with the severest coming in the first mile or so as you leave Pant. The range of countryside makes it very interesting though – ancient quarry and mine workings of the Romans, modern quarrying, then meadows and old railway lines – and there are spectacular views.

Parking

OS Map 126 Ref SJ2722. The bottom of Station Road, by a wide area close to a narrow bridge over the now disused canal.

Further Exploration

The remarkable church in Llanyblodwel is believed to have Norman origins but it was Reverend John Parker who, between 1845 and 1860, rebuilt it with a very Gothic influence and one of the most unusual spires in this country.

Walk up Station Road, cross the main road into Tregarthen Lane and climb, keeping straight at the crossroads and, on reaching a fork with a small post marked 'Water', turn right, walk through a wicker gate and turn sharp left to pass behind the white cottage. On Llanymynech Golf Course, turn right and follow the waymarked signs up a steep climb to the top of the ridge and down the equally steep descent of the path which is now Offa's Dyke. Keep right across the field and turn down the forest track. After a short distance, follow the signs left into a field, over the railway and to the main A495 road. Cross here then, not far from the postbox, climb over a stile and walk up past a bungalow to a narrow lane, where you turn left and head towards Cefn-y-Blodwel. When you reach the driveway to Cefn-y-Blodwel Farm, turn down here and keep right, around the buildings, onto a well-used track which will take you over the ridge and fields, across the valley and up to the main road. Turn left, shortly turning right towards Llanyblodwel, crossing the old packhorse bridge to the pub.

Horseshoe Inn (Marston and Borders)

This is a lovely old-fashioned inn of great character, sitting among other black and white timbered cottages in the village, opposite the narrow bridge over the Afon Tanat. Especially lovely on fine sunny days with picnic benches on the river bank, open fires make it cosy in the winter. Children are welcome during the day and early evening.

On draught: John Marston Premium, Border Mild, Heineken, Guinness and Strongbow cider. Food: The lunch menu includes soup (60p), ploughmans (£1.70), and chicken or sausage and chips (£2.25), whilst the evenings will find more substantial steaks and fish dishes and specials. Telephone: (0691) 828227.

 Cross the pub car park, climb over the gate into a narrow paddock and at the end of this, turn right alongside the hedge to the embankment of a disused railway. Cross the bank, and continue over meadows, two fences and a narrow finger of wood. By the river, continue along the fields to another embankment which you climb before turning right to follow the old railway line. In a little way, you will reach a high red-brick bridge, and should go to the right side to climb up to the road and turn left. Take care as you cross the old railway and the bridges over the river as there are no footpaths. In about ¼ mile, turn sharp right into Green Lane towards Llanymynech Hill. In just over half a mile, the track takes a sharp left turn, then turns right, after which you must turn left, passing under a large oak tree. A little further on, where you find the surface changing to tarmac, turn left and climb past houses and into the wood, back onto Llanymynech Golf Course. There is a waymarked path which takes you round beneath the crags and around the clubhouse, leading you to the road which you take to descend to the A483. Turn left, then right down the narrow lane with the sign indicating a ten ton weight limit, and you will soon be back at your car.

If you still have energy when you return to the golf course, it is worth the climb to the top of the hill where, at the 12th Tee, you will be rewarded by what is virtually a 360 degree view of Shropshire and Wales, a view that is probably unsurpassed anywhere in the Borders.

All Stretton *to* Cardington   Approximately 9 miles

This is a rather strenuous but very rewarding walk, for both the views and the lovely old inn. If you are able to take longer and climb the summits of Caer Caradoc outwards and Willstone Hill on return, the views are superb.

Parking

OS Map 137 SO455944 Car park at the entrance to National Trust area.

Further Exploration

Acton Scott Working Farm Museum, Acton Scott
Just south of Church Stretton on the A49, this old estate farm is now a working museum which gives a vivid account of traditional rural working life. Visitors may take part in some of the work, and there are various craft demonstrations and displays of old machinery and equipment.

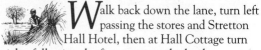

Walk back down the lane, turn left passing the stores and Stretton Hall Hotel, then at Hall Cottage turn right, following the fingerpost, and take the waymarked track over the fields and level crossing to the A49. Cross this very fast main road, turn left and, in a short distance, turn right at the footpath sign and climb the fields to a stile. Turn left onto the waymarked path and start going around Caer Caradoc, climbing gently all the time. Shortly, by a wire fence, keep right and the track gets steeper as it climbs towards the ridge. Go over the fence and head down the slope to the right of the tumulus below. In the corner, you will find a gate and waymarked stile, which will take you up to the top of the field where you turn left onto a drovers track and head towards Willstone. On the way, you will find a poignant memorial to Don Jones of Homer who died while out with the Broseley and Much Wenlock Ramblers on April 24 1988. Keep on down the lane, through Willstone and over the Ford into Cardington, turn left at the signpost, then right and walk around the church to the pub

Royal Oak Inn (Free House)

Built in 1462, this cottage-style pub nestles into the hillside just below the church. The low beams, massive walls and big inglenook fireplace, make it a perfect setting on bleak winter days as well as fine summer ones. Children are welcome, but only if they are eating in the evening.

On draught: Wadworth 6X, Draught Bass, Springfield, Marston Pedigree, Guinness, Carling Black Label, Tennents Extra, Strongbow cider. Food: The ever changing menu is chalked onto a blackboard and contains the usual ploughmans, curry or chicken cobbler (around £2). Food is served at 12-2pm and 7-8.30pm. Closed on Mondays between November and Easter. Telephone: (06943) 266.

*O*ut of the pub, walk up to the right where, in the corner between two cottages, you take the signposted footpath down into fields, over a brook, through a small wood and a couple more fields. Turn right at a big holly tree onto a track up to Hill End Farm. Go around the right side of the buildings and, at the end of the farmyard, turn left up a track to a road. Turn right up to the top of the hill, pass through a gate on your left and walk halfway down the field to a gate. Through this, continue over the next field and through a gate onto a narrow lane where you turn left. Climb up this road, pass North Hill Farm and keep straight ahead onto a waymarked path which will take you over Willstone Hill, just to the left of the summit. At the end of the fence, climb the stile and turn right, descending towards the gate and the brook leading down into a densely wooded valley. Shortly, you will join a good wide vehicle track and, where this crosses the brook, keep to the right-hand side, and continue to the A49. Cross the main road into a lane that leads over the railway, then bear right into the centre of the village. Turn right back to the All Stretton Stores, then left and up the lane back to the car.

Worthen *to* Hopesgate

Approximately 6 miles

This is a walk through valley meadows and hillsides of rich pasture and arable farmland, with some climbing and plenty of fences to negotiate.

Parking

OS Map 126 SJ3204. In front of Worthen Church – space is limited so try the lane alongside or the one opposite

Further Exploration

The villages of Snailbeach, Minsterley and Pontesbury are worth visiting, as well as the brooding Stiperstones which can be seen from many parts of the walk.

*F*ollow the lane by the church and over the waymarked stile into meadows, keeping alongside the brook on the left, then cross the footbridge. At the end of a wooden fence, cross the brook by another footbridge and follow the waymarked stiles up to the road, into which you turn left. In ¾ mile, a footpath sign on the right will take you around Bank Farm. After crossing the farm entrance track and its next field, ignore the stile down into the wooded gorge as storm damage has lost the path. Instead, keep between the wood and the wire fence down into the corner of the field where you can walk along the brook until you climb the fence and then turn left up the side of the wood. Keep to the side of this wood, the ditch and the hedge, heading up to the top corner where, by a water-trough, you pass through the gate, cross the field on the well-defined track skirting Lady House Farm, and aim to the right of the motte – the sugar lump mound topped with about three trees. Just beyond this is the road into which you turn right, pass the entrance to Hope Hall on your left, and you will soon approach the pub, also on your left.

*T*urn left out of the pub, turning right into a field and head for the right side of the red-brick bulk of Leigh Manor by following the old track down the hill skirting the wood. As you reach a farm, go through the gate and turn sharp left up the hill to another gate, and through a narrow piece of wood into a small paddock, the other side of which will be a road. Turn right and descend to a black barn, where you turn left and pass through the gates. Follow the cart tracks which take you down the field then climb the hillside to a gate at the top of Whitsburn Hill. Go straight down the hill now quite steeply, to a track which takes you to the road. Turn left and, after the narrow little bridge over the Rea Brook, climb the stile on the right, and a series of further stiles, all waymarked, will lead you back into Worthen.

Stables Inn (Free House)

This is an attractive and appealing small inn, fully carpeted, with lots of beams and a good display of mugs, loving cups and other bric-a-brac. Built in 1720, it served the drovers on the high route between Montgomery and Shrewsbury, who avoided the toll bridges in the valleys. The most striking resident today is the huge ginger tom, aptly named Whingey. Children are welcome at lunchtimes only.

On draught: Ind Coope Burton, Marston Pedigree, Wood Porter, Hanby Drawwell, Beamish, Skol, Lowenbrau, Weston's cider, Old Rosie Extra Strong Scrumpy. Food: Served in the three small sitting areas or the tiny dining room, the menu includes some interesting dishes, such as beef, Irish stout and walnut casserole, haddock and prawn crumble, and cheese, tomato and aubergine bake. Bar meals at lunchtime can start at £1.50, while the average for three courses in the evening will be about £8.50. Food is served at 12-2pm and 6.30-9pm (Thursday to Saturday only, or other nights by appointment). Closed Mondays except Bank Holidays. Booking advisable. Telephone: (0743) 891344.

Colstey Wood *to* Clun

Approximately 7 miles

This walk is quite hilly, so be prepared for some climbing and you will be rewarded with peace and tranquility – 'Clunton and Clunbury, Clungunford and Clun are the quietest places under the sun.'(A E Housman, A Shropshire Lad)

Parking
OS Map 137 Ref SO3084 The wide entrance to the Forestry Commission's Colstey Wood.

*T*ake the forest walk through the gate then very shortly, keep slightly left with the track descending into the forest. Keep on this track until you pass a small pool, shortly after which you turn sharp right. In ¼ mile, look for a green marked post and turn right onto a well-defined path. Through a gate, the path will eventually become a metalled road. At a large grey house, turn right and this road will take you to Clun. At the little hospital, turn right and then immediately left. On reaching the main road, turn right to the pub.

Sun Inn (Free House)

 This 15th-century building of cruck construction has a wealth of dark beams and is furnished with Windsor chairs, stools and settle seating plus lots of bric-à-brac, give a warm atmosphere which is helped along by friendly staff and locals.

On draught: Banks's Bitter and Mild, Wood Special, guest beers such as Wadworth 6X and Taylors Landlord. There is also a small but inexpensive wine list. Food: A small menu for bar meals of the expected sandwiches, ploughmans and basket meals is supplemented by daily specials such as cashew nut paella, Mexican bean pot, and gammon with orange and lemon sauce (all around £5.50). Food is served at 12-2pm and 7-9pm. Telephone: (05884) 559 or 277.

*T*urn right out of the pub into the square, and turn right into Bishops Castle road. At the corner of the grey walls, turn left towards the castle but before you reach the castle grounds, go over a stile to your right into a green lane. Walk down into the field alongside the hedge, through a gap and, in the corner, over another stile up onto a narrow lane by the local coal merchant. Keep by the hedge and alongside the River Unk, over a footbridge and follow the well-defined footpath behind Hawthorns, passing earthworks to a road where you turn right to the village of Bicton. At the far end of the village, a waymarked path to the left ascends a scrub-covered hill, passing a small recent quarry. Keep with the track to the left of a wood, following it up until it gradually peters out. Climb over the gate ahead of you and down the side of a field to a narrow road where you turn right then, at a T-junction, turn left onto the main road, which is the A488 again, over the hill to your car.

Further Exploration
Clun has a small museum in the Town Hall, and other interests are the Parish Church of St George and the 17th-century Trinity Hospital. Nearby is Offa's Dyke and many other peaceful villages of the Clun Valley which once resounded to the many battles against the Romans and also between the English and Welsh who long disputed ownership of the area. Relics of this stormy past, such as Norman Mottes and other ancient earthworks, can be found throughout the area.

Itteringham *to* Blickling
Approximately 6 miles

A gentle walk through farming land and parkland – watch out for badgers and rabbits.

Parking
OS Map 133 Ref TG1431 By the church.

Further Exploration.
Blickling Hall
This 17th-century house is just across the road from the pub and flanked by hedges that could be even older than the house itself. The most celebrated room is the Long Gallery, whose 125ft long ceiling is covered in ornate Jacobean plasterwork, but other attractions include the Chinese wallpaper, hand painted in the 18th century, the 17th-century Mortlake tapestries and, of course, the 43 acres of grounds. Telephone: (0263) 733084.

From the church, head south along the road until you reach a junction. A lane goes left, while a white gate crosses the next lane, also to the left. On the post, there is a yellow arrow pointing straight, so go through, past the house, and through another gate into a leafy lane. At the end of the lane there is another gate leading to a wide clearing. Keep to the right, following the woods round, and you'll reach another gate and stile. Continue through two cow fields, and at the third head towards the small wooden bridge straight ahead. Cross this, then turn left and immediately cross another, larger bridge over the river. Vegetation is quite wild at this point, so be prepared to tread down a few nettles and brambles. Make your way from the bridge to a gate which brings you to a quiet lane, into which you turn left. Follow this lane as far as a sharp curve to the left, where you'll find an entrance to Blickling Park. There are a number of paths through the park – keep heading east on the main track (Weaver's Way) with the tower always on your right, until you reach the exit to Blickling. Leaving the park, turn left and follow the narrow lane round to the pub.

Buckinghamshire Arms (Free House)

This fine country inn built in 1693, is a Grade II listed building and owned by the National Trust. It has a snug bar whose walls are covered with brass tap fittings and old pictures, and a larger lounge with cosy alcoves and comfortable seats. Outside there are several large trestle tables, behind the ivy-covered building, plenty of grass to sit on, and a children's play area.

On draught: Adnams, Greene King Abbot and IPA, Flower's Original, Guinness, Woodford's Norfolk Wherry, Carlsberg, Carlsberg Export. Food: A basic menu offers generous portions of freshly prepared meals including jacket potatoes with various fillings, sandwiches and ploughmans, ranging from £1.60 - £4. Food is served at 12-2.30pm and 7-10pm (restaurant 7-9.30pm). Telephone: (0263) 732133.

*R*etrace your steps to Blickling Park, and take the right fork in the path. Follow this long stretch until the path curves around to the left. Keep going straight along a grassy path between the fields, and follow this path around past some houses onto a road. Turn left and continue along the road until it bends sharply to the right. There you will see a track to your right signposted to Weaver's Way, which takes you along the river bank, over a small wooden bridge and along a narrow track overhung with branches. Where it turns into a tarmaced road, turn left into a wide farm track through the field. Keep on this track, past the farm buildings, until it eventually curves to the left. Keep going straight along the side of the field (there is an arrow on a post pointing the way), climb over the stile, and bear left along the next field until you reach another stile which brings you to the clearing you passed on your outward route. Pass through the gate opposite and retrace your steps along the leafy lane, through the two gates, to Itteringham, turning right towards the church.

St Mary's Church, Itteringham
The church is reputed to be the work of Aymer de Valens, who rebuilt several churches in the area in the 13th century. There is a substantial square tower where originally, there were three bells, but in 1824 the largest and smallest were sold to pay for roof repairs, fetching £72. An extract of a record of the collapse of the bellgallows in 1601, hangs by the bellrope. The interior was redesigned in 1859 and the box pews date from this time, but the poppy heads on the bench ends are much older.

West Acre *to* Castle Acre   Approximately 5½ miles

A gentle walk through farm and woodland, with views of the magnificent priory ruins at Castle Acre. In summer, you may see some lovely scenes of local children playing in the fords, although ideally, this is a spring or autumn walk.

Parking

OS Map 132 Ref TF7915
Parking area at the corner of a lane opposite Mill House.

Further Exploration

Castle Acre has a very pretty, tree-lined main road, with two pubs, a post office, tea rooms and a newsagent. It seems very lively for such a small place, but this is clearly due to the attraction of the priory ruins.

*Castle Acre Priory
(National Trust)*
Built for the Clunaic order by Earl Warren, son-in-law of William the Conqueror, the priory fell into ruin after the Dissolution in 1536. Rising above the extensive remains is the glorious arcaded west front of the priory church, a reminder of past splendour.

Cross over the lane, down which you will see a ford, and take the next lane which passes to the right of Mill House. Follow this until you reach a copse on your right, and turn right up along it's edge. Follow this round to the left, until you reach a track. Turn right and continue along this pleasant path – trying to ignore the pylon – past another wooded area to your right, rife with rabbits and partridges, up to a turning on your left. Follow this along the edge of the field, turning left again at a junction of paths and continue down to the road. Turn right and pass the old flint house and the disused church before turning left at a fork, and then left again. This road takes you across a ford and up past the priory remains. At the top of the road, turn right into the village of Castle Acre, and you will soon see the pub on your left.

Leave the pub, turn right and retrace your steps as far as the church and South Acre Road. Continue straight, past the entrance to the priory, and follow the road round to the right. At the next bend, there is a wide track on your left. Follow this downhill as far as a gate which leads to a field as the track bears to the right. Go through the gate and follow the path around the edge of the field until you reach a stile on your right beneath the trees. Over the stile, this path takes you through the shady wood to a gate and a meadow. Follow the track diagonally across the meadow, bearing right, and join the grassy path which leads you to a small bridge, and a stile. Continue along the path to another bridge and then a final stile which brings you to the road by the ford. Turn left to return to your car.

Ostrich (Greene King)

This large, rambling old pub has a spacious, yet cosy front bar beyond which is the eating area. This family room, with its high ceiling, brickwork, beams and open fire, suggests that the building may once have been an old hall. There is a door to the garden which has plenty of picnic tables, and a hutch of rabbits. The staff are all welcoming and efficient.

On draught: Greene King IPA and Abbot Ale, Kronenbourg 1666, Fosters, Taunton's cider. Food: The food is well presented and very good value. Look for specials on the blackboard above the bar – these are often vegetarian meals. Menu includes a variety of ploughmans (from £1.70) and sandwiches (from 70p), omelettes (from £1.40), steak meals (from £6.00), basket meals (from £2.50) and pizzas (from £1.40). Vegetarian choices include spinach and cheese roll and vegetable terrine (both £2.50). Food is served from 12-2pm and 7-10.30pm. Telephone: (0760) 755398.

Holme next the Sea
to Thornham

Approximately 6 miles.

An easy and interesting coastal walk alongside the North Holme Nature Reserve. Watch out for rare species of migratory birds.

Parking

OS Map 132 Ref TF6944 (50p per day)

Further Exploration

Holme Nature Reserve
This is administered by the Norfolk Naturalists Trust and non-members are required to pay an entry fee. Varied habitats include dunes, saltmarsh, brackish, and fresh water pools, which make this site a paradise for a range of wildlife. Permits may be obtained to visit the Holme Bird Observatory Reserve which was established in 1962 on seven acres of pine and scrub-covered dunes, and where the study of migratory birds is carried out daily. There are five hides available for use by visitors, and there is a ten-post nature trail designed for families, a nature garden and a pond. Telephone: (048525) 240.

 *L*eave the car park from the entrance and bear right, heading towards the sea. When you reach the path running along the coast, at a slightly higher level than the beach, turn right. This path is marked with yellow arrows, and there are information signs at various points along the route telling you about the reserve and the flora and fauna to be seen. Follow the path along the coast and then inland as you approach Thornham. When the path meets a road used by yachtsmen and others visiting the small marina, turn right and the pub is straight ahead.

When you leave the pub, you can go back along the same path, or return along the beach.

Lifeboat Inn (Free House)

Built in the late 1500's, this pub has a well-documented history of offering a warm haven to smugglers and travellers alike. The two small bars have low ceilings, beams and dark wooden furniture, and there is a large eating area at the back, a separate restaurant, and a courtyard with many picnic tables and a play area for children. Situated next to a campsite, this pub gets extremely busy during the summer, especially at weekends.

On draught: Greene King IPA and Abbot Ale, Tolly Cobbold, Harp, Carlsberg, Strongbow cider. Food: There is a very wide range of snacks and main meals, served in generous portions. The menu includes sandwiches (from £1.45), ploughmans (£3.25), chicken with mushroom, bacon and cream sauce (£4.95), and vegetarian lasagne (£4.25). Desserts (all £1.75) include hot ginger sponge and butterscotch and walnut gateau. There is also a separate children's menu. Food is served at 12-2.15pm and 7-10pm. The restaurant opens at 7.30pm, but booking is essential. Telephone: (048526) 236.

Minsmere *to* Eastbridge

Approximately 5 miles

Start your walk from the back of the car park, taking the track nearest the public convenience building and head downhill towards the water. Follow the path away from the sea, through the woods, following the curve of the water but keeping it to your left. At a T-junction, turn left, cross a stile and head towards another junction. Turn left again, and when you reach a road, cross straight over and continue along the track up and down Hangman's Hill. When the path joins the road, keep straight to arrive at the pub.

A delightful walk which takes you through farmland, woodland, heathland and along the seashore. If you take your binoculars you may see some rare birds, as the route borders the Minsmere Nature Reserve.

The Eel's Foot (Adnams)

This is a very small, unpretentious pub with friendly staff and a happy, relaxed atmosphere. There are lots of tables in the garden, and swings for the active.

On draught: Adnams, Murphys Stout, Carling Black Label, Lowenbrau and Strongbow cider. Food: A basic menu includes cottage pie (£3.10), steak and kidney pie (£3.00) and sausage and chips (£2.10) Food is served at 11.45-2pm and 6-11pm. Telephone: (0728) 830154.

Parking
OS Map 156 Ref TM4767
National Trust car park (£1, free to members).

Further Exploration
Minsmere Nature Reserve (RSPB)
This bird sanctuary is the most important in Europe. For non-members, there is a public hide whose entrance is near The Sluice - don't forget your binoculars!

Dunwich Cliffs
This is a popular spot for hang-gliders, but for the less adventurous there is the National Trust Shop and Tea Rooms.

Turn left out of the pub, and you will soon see a sign pointing left and indicating 'To the Sluice'. Follow this path through farmland straight down to the sea. At the shore, turn left and, depending on the weather, you can either walk along the shore or behind the dunes. Sometimes parts of the dunes are roped off while birds are breeding, so you will have to take the beach. Head towards the white National Trust building on the cliff, and you will soon be back at the car park.

Eastbridge *to* Westleton

Approximately 5 miles

Parking

OS Map 156 Ref TM4566
Clearing under some trees just
north of the bridge, and south of
the entrance to Minsmere
Nature Reserve.

Further Exploration

Westleton is a lovely village,
with a duck pond, a craft shop
and a second-hand book shop
inside an old church hall.

Walk back to the bridge and turn right immediately after crossing it. This footpath runs along the riverbank. Be sure to follow this rather than the track through the field – you can't change paths later on as they are separated by stretches of water. When you reach a road, turn right and walk a short distance along it before taking the next bridleway on your right. This gorse-lined path slopes gently up to the Westleton road, into which you turn left and walk into the village. At the main street, turn right and you will soon arrive at the pub.

Crown (Free House)

The cosy bars of this very spacious and welcoming pub, have an interesting assortment of old farming tools and photographs of village scenes on the walls. There is also an elegent orangerie and large pretty, terraced patio with plenty of seating, and a garden with picnic tables. Children are made welcome - they even have a special menu.

On draught: Adnams Southwold and Broadside, Sam Smith's, Whitbread Best, Wadworth 6X, Badger Best, Tuborg Gold, Carlsberg and James White's Suffolk Cider. Food: An imaginative menu includes sandwiches and soup (both from £1), duck, venison and pork in port (£7.25) and grilled whole sole (£3.95). Telephone: (072873) 273.

Leiston Abbey
This 14th-century ruin is less than a mile from Eastbridge. The remains of the choir and transepts of the church, and the ranges of cloisters still stand, and cream teas are available in summer in the Georgian mansion.

*T*urn right out of the pub then right again at Bakers Lane, opposite the craft shop. This will lead you to the junction where you joined the road on the outward journey. Follow the footpath sign rather than Budle Way, walking through farmland and a wood before you reach a vehicle barrier to a track which then meets a road. To the left is the entrance to Minsmere, and straight ahead should be your car.

Iken to Snape

Approximately 5 miles.

A gentle walk by the River Alde, with pretty views of marshes and saltings. Avocets can often be seen as well as oyster-catchers, shellduck, grebe, the occasional marsh harrier, and many more river birds.

Parking

OS Map 156 Ref TM4056. Iken Cliffs car park.

Further Exploration

Snape Maltings

This is a unique collection of Victorian industrial buildings, originally used to malt barley, now having various craft, kitchen and garden shops, an art gallery, restaurant and tea shop. The renowned music school and concert hall, set up by Sir Peter Pears and Sir Benjamin Britten, is also to be found here. In the summer there is a programme of activity holidays, and river trips from Snape Quay are a relaxing way to see the river and its wildlife. Telephone: (072888) 303.

Aldeburgh

This delightful seaside town is only a few minutes away by car. There are some beautiful buildings, a charming seafront, and an interesting Moot Hall Museum.

*B*egin your walk by finding the footpath at the bottom left-hand corner of the car park. This is mainly a planked path of railway sleepers, and it runs beside the marshes with farmland to the left and the river to the right. When you reach a fork in the path, keep to the left until you reach a road. There, turn right and walk past the front of Snape Maltings and over the bridge. Turn right immediately after the bridge and follow the river wall to some woods and a yellow footpath sign. At this point, you may like to turn right and wander down to the river's edge, but make sure you return to this spot. Turn left at the sign (or straight on if you have been down to the river), then left again into a path which opens up on one side to give you views across the marshes to Snape Maltings. At the end of this stretch of path – called The Canser – turn right and you will shortly reach a road. Turn left and the pub is on the next corner.

*T*urn left out of the pub and follow the road back towards Snape Maltings. Having crossed over the bridge, turn immediately left and follow the path at the back of the Maltings, past the bronze sculpture, and head towards the avenue of trees. There are two paths to the left of this avenue one running parallel to it, and one running at right angles. The latter follows the water's edge and does bring you back to the car park, but is only possible at low tide. Take the former, follow it as far as a T-junction and turn left towards the car park.

Crown Inn (Adnams)

 This is a super pub with lots of room inside and out. Wooden beams and old pine furniture add to the comfortable, relaxed atmosphere inside, while the garden is more lively, with a number of farmyard animals living at one end. The landlord and his staff are all very helpful and friendly.

On draught: Stocks vary with the seasons; normally you will find Best, Southwold, Broadside, Fosters and Murphys Old Stout, with the addition of Mild and Tally Ho in winter, and a good cider in the summer. Food: Meals are all freshly made, and seafood features in many of the good value dishes, all of which are served in generous portions. Meals include seafood pancakes (£3.95), chicken and avocado salad (£3.95), lasagne verdi (£4.95) and lamb cutlets (£4.95), with a range of desserts (£1.65) from strawberries and ice cream to pear and almond flan. Food is served everyday throughout the lunchtime session, and from 6pm every evening. Telephone: (072888) 324.

Polstead *to* Stoke-by-Nayland

Approximately 5 miles.

A pretty and varied walk through open meadows, copses, and leafy lanes, incorporating two deceptively tranquil villages which, between them, have a fascinating history of witches, murder, and treason.

Parking
OS Map 155 Ref TL9938
Outside Polstead village hall.

Further Exploration.
A small detour up Martin's Lane before returning to the green, will bring you to the former home of Maria Marten, victim of the famous Murder in The Red Barn in 1827. Her body is buried in the churchyard of St Mary's.

Stoke-by-Nayland is a pretty village of splendid timber-framed and lath and plaster buildings. It was once the home of Thomas Hood who was beheaded by Queen Elizabeth for trying to marry Mary Queen of Scots and filch the crown. Its church has a marvellous tower of 120 ft in height, much painted by Constable, and is a famous landmark for miles around.

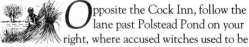

Opposite the Cock Inn, follow the lane past Polstead Pond on your right, where accused witches used to be 'swum' and into which once a coach and four horses, having been bewitched, plunged headlong. Go directly across the road to the clearly marked footpath which bears left and curves across a pretty meadow, past St Mary's Church – a Norman structure with the distinction of having the oldest surviving English bricks. Reaching a quiet road, turn right and cross a narrow part of the river over a small bridge, before taking the footpath on the left, signposted to Scotland Street, along the edge of a meadow and through a farmyard to a quiet lane. Turn right and follow the lane to some crossroads, and the pub is directly ahead.

Angel Inn (Free House)

This pub, with its low ceilings and wooden beams, is surprisingly light and airy. The rooms are furnished mainly with plain wooden chairs and tables, but one section has large comfortable armchairs in a cosy group. Paintings of local scenes adorn the brick walls, and outside there is a a small patio garden with a few sheltered tables. Superb food and charming staff combine to make this a very popular establishment. Well-behaved children are welcome inside, in the eating area.

On draught: Greene King IPA and Abbot Ale, Adnams, Bass, Kronenbourg 1664, Carlsberg, Taunton's cider. Food: Excellent dishes are beautifully presented and range from deep fried brie in filo pastry with strawberry and pepper sauce (£3.75), to baked lamb Bolangere with salad (£5.75) and rainbow trout, salad and chips (£7.25). Puddings include cream crowdie (£2.50) and white chocolate and orange terrine (£2.45). Food is served at 12-2pm and 6.30-9pm. Sunday 12-1.30pm and 7-9pm. Telephone: (0206) 263245.

Turn right out of the inn and continue along this road for a short distance before taking a footpath along the side of a field on your left. This path goes down to a stile on your left which you should pass, carrying on uphill for a short way. At a clearing, the path forks, so keep to the left and carry on down towards the farm buildings across the next field. You will come out on the farm track which curves round from the right. Go straight until you reach Longs Bridge on your left – opposite the first building – and cross this, following the main track straight ahead. On reaching a fork in the path, bear left and carry on until you reach the road. Turn left and follow this road straight until you reach a gateway on the left, with a footpath sign just off the road. Follow this path towards the farm buildings, but before you reach them, go over a stile on your right, and follow the track through the trees. There are yellow arrows directing you all the way through the wood, so watch out for them. At a clearing, bear right, and then left again when you reach a signpost pointing in four directions. Keep following the yellow arrows to the quiet lane at the end of the wood. Turn left into the lane and follow it down towards Polstead. Keep right when it forks, and take the narrow footpath immediately on your right which leads you over a stile, past some donkeys, through a wide gate, up between some houses, and back to Polstead Green.

Trimley St Martin *to* Trimley St Mary

Approximately 4 miles

An easy, level walk following a figure of eight through farmland. There are splendid views of the River Orwell, up past the pretty marina at Levington towards Pin Mill, across to Shotley and Harwich, and down to Felixstowe Docks.

Parking

OS Map 169 Ref TM2734. Memorial hall car park just off the High Street.

Further information

For those wishing to extend their walk along the shore, a diversion upstream will take you past Loompit Lake to Levington Marina. Alternatively, turn down towards Felixstowe and you will soon come to the Suffolk Wildlife Reserve.

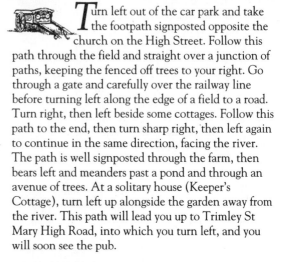

Turn left out of the car park and take the footpath signposted opposite the church on the High Street. Follow this path through the field and straight over a junction of paths, keeping the fenced off trees to your right. Go through a gate and carefully over the railway line before turning left along the edge of a field to a road. Turn right, then left beside some cottages. Follow this path to the end, then turn sharp right, then left again to continue in the same direction, facing the river. The path is well signposted through the farm, then bears left and meanders past a pond and through an avenue of trees. At a solitary house (Keeper's Cottage), turn left up alongside the garden away from the river. This path will lead you up to Trimley St Mary High Road, into which you turn left, and you will soon see the pub.

Three Mariners (Norwich)

This busy, friendly pub has a spacious and comfortable lounge bar, a separate eating area and a public bar which is simply furnished and decorated along a nautical theme. A children's room is planned for the summer of 1991. Outside, there are chairs and tables on the patio and benches on the lawn which also has a children's play area. Dogs are allowed only in the public bar.

On draught: Norwich, Webster's Yorkshire, Ruddles Best, Adnams, Guinness, Holstein Export, Carlsberg, Fosters, Strongbow cider. Food: Locally renowned for good value, home-cooked meals and snacks, the menu includes generous portions of delicious home cooked ham, sirloin steak, Mariner's Grill (sausage, steak, bacon and lamb chop), breaded lemon sole filled with crabmeat in a seafood sauce, vegetable strogonoff, coconut and sultana curry and various omelettes, salads and sandwiches. Prices range from £1 to £6.50. Food is served at 12-2pm and 7.30-10pm. Telephone: (0394) 284767.

Turn left out of the pub and take the next turning on the left, Gun Lane. This road soon turns into a path across the field to a gate providing access across the railway line. Continue along this path for a short distance, but before you reach the second telegraph pole, take the footpath on your right, across the field towards two semi-detached cottages. (If the field is too muddy to cross, go down to the lane as you did earlier and turn right up to the junction, where you bear left.) At the cottages, turn left then right at the junction, heading towards a cottage with a mansard roof. Just past this is a wide footpath to the right which you follow across the field to a junction. At this point, you might enjoy a detour down to the river, so turn left here for the shore. Otherwise, turn right and follow the track, which becomes a road, through the farmyard and along the lane past a few houses before you reach a junction. Take the footpath straight ahead, keeping to the left of the field before going straight through the middle of the field, crossing a lane and continuing between two gardens to the railway line. Cross and continue straight before taking the first footpath to the left, back to Trimley St Martin High Street and your car behind the church.

Manningtree *to* Dedham   Approximately 6 miles

A popular walk through the countryside which inspired the artist Constable to paint some of his finest and best-known works. The walk is very clearly signposted.

Parking

OS Map 168 Ref TM0932, Manningtree railway station.

Further Exploration

Dedham

It is well worth dawdling round this pretty village before resuming your walk. Look out for the Elizabethan Free School, and the 16th-century church whose tower can be found in many of Constable's paintings. Sir Alfred Munnings, President of the Royal Academy from 1944-1949, also lived here and his house is now a gallery dedicated to his work.

Walk back to the road from the car park and almost double back on your tracks to follow a public footpath running parallel to the railway line. After a short distance, turn left up the side of a field and follow the clearly marked path round to the right. Follow it into the churchyard and turn right when you reach the road. Turn left fairly soon, keeping the handsome red brick facade of Lawford Hall on your right. At the bottom of the track, turn left into the road and right after a few yards up the public footpath. Walk down the side of the field on your right, not by the fruit trees on the left, which are private. Follow the path straight ahead and it leads to a rough road. Take the right hand fork and go over the railway line, keeping Hill Farm on your right. Cross the road and follow the public footpath ahead until it meets another small road. Follow this as it bends round to the right and then to the left. Turn right at the next small crossroads and you will have a short walk into Dedham.

Marlborough Head (Ind Coope)

Set in the beautiful 'Constable country', and opposite the painter's old school, this is a delightfully unspoilt 15th-century pub with several bars. There is some fine carved woodwork in the central lounge, and the Constable bar is beamed and furnished with wooden tables in alcoves. There is a garden with a patio and a children's play area.

On draught: Adnams, Benskins Best, John Bull, Guinness and Lowenbrau. There are 18 wines on offer, ranging in price from £6.50 to £15.50 a bottle. Food: The menu is vast and varied and includes cream cheese and caviar sandwich (£2.50), ploughmans (£2.50), and rabbit casserole (£4.50). Several vegetarian dishes are always on offer, such as pine kernel and pumpkin seed risotto (£3.75). Delicious desserts include chocolate and brandy pot (£2.50) and fresh nectarine melba with cream (£2.25). All the food is fresh and the service is quick, friendly and efficient, even when busy. Food is served at 12-2pm and 7-9.30pm. Telephone: (0206) 323124.

Out of the pub, retrace your steps out of the village. At the right hand bend, bear left up the public footpath and follow this down to the river. Climb over two stiles and turn right when you reach the river. Keep the water on your left at all times. Climb through two horizontal metal bars (erected to stop cows, not people) and follow the river for about 2½ miles. Follow the steps down and up a redundant concrete lock and turn left on to a grass track. Climb two stiles, turning sharp right after the second. Turn left at the bottom of the path and follow the lane round to the right. Walk under the railway, then turn left up the track towards the car park of Manningtree station.

Flatford Mill

Once the Constable family mill, this now belongs to the National Trust and houses one of the centres organised and administered by the Field Study Council. It is not open to the public, but large groups can arrange in advance to be shown around.

Next to the mill is The Bridge Cottage (NT), which has a visitors centre, information on John Constable, a tea room and a shop. Telephone: (0206) 298260.

Willy Lott's Cottage is one of Constable's most celebrated subjects. Once the home of a friend of the painter, it has been meticulously preserved, and remains a private house.

If you wish to see the countryside from a different angle, skiffs, rowing boats and canoes can be hired from The Bridge Cottage or the boatyard in Mill Lane, Dedham, every day of the week between Easter and October.

Clavering *to* Arkesden   Approximately 6 miles

An easy, mainly flat walk through typical Essex countryside, passing through two of the county's prettiest villages.

Parking

OS Map 167 Ref TL4731 behind the Fox & Hounds pub, Clavering.

Further Exploration

Audley End House
This is an English Heritage property just west of Saffron Walden and well worth a visit. It is an impressive stone building with beautifully landscaped gardens, where open air productions are often held in the summer. Telephone: (0799) 22399.

*T*ake the gravel drive behind the Fox & Hounds pub, cross on to the grass and head for the stile ahead. Climb up the hill, turning left before you reach the top, and head for the house at the bottom. The public footpath goes round to the left of the house as you approach it. Follow the gravel path to the road and turn right. Bear left when you reach The Cricketers pub and follow the road to Arkesden, keeping the pub on your right. Turn left down the side of a field beyond the houses. The public footpath turns left and you will see Wood Hall ahead of you. Go round the back of the house, where the footpath points towards Arkesden. The path to the village takes you almost up the back garden of the pub.

Axe and Compasses (Greene King)

This very popular pub has three separate areas – a comfortable main bar with armchairs, an adjoining dining area which has original beams and small vases of flowers on the tables, and a separate bar with a dartboard and bare floor. The pub is part-thatched and has an outside seating area with attractive, rustic garden furniture, overlooking the village post office and shop.

On draught: Greene King IPA and Abbot Ale, Kronenbourg 1664. There is a good selection of wine by the glass or bottle. Food: Typical dishes, which are homemade, include soup of the day (£1.40) or egg mayonnaise (£1.60) for starters, followed by steak and kidney pie (£4.95), lamb cutlets (£5.95) or cottage pie (£3.95). There are a variety of pies and cheesecakes for dessert. Vegetarians can choose from nut roast, vegetarian lasagne and stuffed aubergines. There are barbecues in the garden on Sundays during the summer. Food is served at 12-2pm and 1-9.30pm. Booking advisable. Telephone: (0799) 550272.

Turn left out of the pub and follow the narrow main road through Arkesden. After a short distance, take the public footpath on the left, signposted to Chardwell Farm. Go straight on at the first arrowed post, round the edge of the field and turn right at the next post in the corner of the field. Walk over a two-plank footbridge and round Chardwell Farm. This path can become rather overgrown in the summer. Turn left at the next arrowed post into a dip, keeping the stream on your left. Climb over the next stile, and follow the left-hand side of the field until you reach a small copse. Bear left up the bridlepath and you will soon reach a rough road. Turn left and walk into the farmyard, then take the metalled road off to the right. Turn right when you reach the main road and walk past a disused flour mill, then take the path by the side of the field immediately after Mill Cottage on the left. This may not be signposted, but is clearly a public footpath. Walk down the side of this field and turn right at the bottom, where you will see the village of Clavering nestling in the hollow. Climb over two stiles to reach the road. It is worth crossing the road in front of you to have a look at the beautiful, tiny thatched cottages and a larger Tudor house ahead. Follow the road round to the left and on to the main road and you will see the Fox and Hounds pub a few yards away.

Toppesfield *to* Delvin End   Approximately 5 miles

A very pretty, and easy, walk through farmland. Watch out for herons and migratory birds.

Parking

OS Map 155 Ref TL7337 The middle of Toppesfield, near the church.

Further Exploration

Hedingham Castle
Built in 1130, the castle has a keep which is one of the best of its date in England, and which stands 100 ft high. The banqueting hall and minstrel's gallery are among other features in good condition. Telephone: (0787) 60261.

Colne Valley Railway & Museum
There are seven steam locomotives here, in steam from June to December. Telephone: (0787) 61174.

*F*rom the pump in the centre of the village, take the direction of the signpost to Great Yeldham. Between two houses (numbers 9 and 11), take the unmarked footpath through an allotment, then beside a hedge to a road. Keep on the path as it continues left on the high grass verge beside the road. As you approach Toppesfield Hall on the left and Oliver's Farm on the right, look for the footpath which runs down the side of the farm, to your right. It is marked, but easy to miss. Past the farmhouse, bear right through a gap and join a concrete path. Close to a barn, just to the right of the farmhouse, take the clear path which runs at right angles to the pylon lines – it is about midway between two sets of pylons. (Do not follow the track to the left by the woods.) Follow the path downhill to the bottom, then cross into the field on the right, following the track and keeping the stream to your left. You will soon cross the stream and reach a junction of paths. Turn left and follow this path round to the right, where it becomes a concrete path. Climb up this path to a road and turn left. Follow this road over a junction, past a few houses, to the pub.

Bottlehall (Free House)

The unusual name of this former blacksmith and off licence, comes from a time when the government imposed a tax on the number of windows in a building. The owner used bottles to block up his windows in order to avoid paying the tax and still manage to steal a little light. Three of the windows are still blocked in this way. The two bars and small restaurant are cosy and welcoming, and there are picnic benches outside for eating out fine weather. Children are welcome in the restaurant.

On draught: Greene King IPA and XX Mild, and a guest beer (all served straight from the barrel), Kronenbourg 1664, Fosters, Carlsberg. Food: Traditional meals are home made and include Irish stew, hotpot, and various pies as well as the usual ploughmans and sandwiches. Meals average around £5. Food is served all day. Telephone: (0787) 62405.

*T*urn left out of the pub, soon taking the marked footpath to your left, beside the garden of a house. When you reach a field, turn right and walk around the edge of the field to the opposite side, where you cross into the next field. The pub should be almost directly behind you, and a house and some barns are to your right. Continue along this way until you reach a road, into which you turn right. Directly opposite the semi-detached brick houses, follow the footpath through more farm and woodland, keeping straight on until you reach another road. Turn left and follow the road for a short distance before turning left into a farm driveway marked with a footpath sign. Follow the path as it bears right in the centre of the farm buildings and follows an old railway track to a road. Turn left and walk along this road until you turn right at a footpath to Scotneys. This path leads directly into Toppesfield, past the church and back to the village pump.

Ashdon *to* Bartlow   Approximately 6 miles

A gently undulating walk through well-worn tracks which afford good views of the Essex and Cambridgeshire countryside.

Parking

OS Map 154 Ref TL5841 In the lane leading up to All Saints' Church.

Further exploration

Linton Zoological Gardens
The zoo has been operating since 1972 and has a large collection of leopards, pumas, panthers, vultures, macaws, snakes, bird-eating spiders and many other creatures.
Telephone: (0223) 891308.

St Mary's Church, Bartlow, dates from the 14th century and has an unusual rounded Norman tower.

Walk round to the left of the churchyard, climb the stile into the field behind and walk down the hill. Over the stile at the bottom of the field, turn left down the track to the road. Cross, and walk on the footpath on the other side. Turn right and follow the road towards Ashdon. When the footpath meets the road, cross and follow the public footpath sign to the right. Walk over the plank bridge, straight ahead and between the posts marked with yellow bands, towards the road. Turn left when you reach the road, then right again fairly soon, up Kate's Lane. After about ½ mile, turn left on the public footpath across the field towards the windmill in the distance. Turn right at the top of the field, left at the corner, then join the narrow road between the houses and the windmill down to the main road. Turn right at the road, then left through white gates and up a gravel drive. When the drive bears right towards two houses, follow the footpath straight on. At a junction of paths, take the grassiest track straight ahead. At the corner of the field, turn left down the slope, then right. This track meets a rough road, into which you turn left. Keep left at the first fork and turn right just before you meet the road. Round the back of Hills Farm, keep parallel to the road and bear right over the disused railway line, straight on and through the churchyard. At the road, turn left, then left again at the crossroads to the pub.

Three Hills (Greene King)

 This is a large, handsome pub whose comfortable bar features an inglenook fireplace, and fresh flowers on the tables. There is also a well-kept garden. A popular establishment, it soon becomes busy, but the service is well organised and friendly.

On draught: Greene King Abbot Ale and IPA, Rayment BBA, Kronenbourg 1664. Food: For starters, try salmon and halibut terrine (£2.95) or soup of the day. Main courses include a seafood platter or chicken and new potatoes (both £4.95), and desserts include walnut fool, strawberry tart or fresh cheesecake. A special menu for vegetarians is always available, there is a barbecue in the garden on sunny summer Sundays, and roasts are served on winter Sundays. Food is served at 12-1.45pm and 7-9.30pm. Telephone: (0223) 891259.

*T*urn left on to the road after leaving the pub and take the first road right towards Hadstock. Walk under the disused railway line and take the track off to the left ½ mile later. Go straight on at the first fork and bear left at the second. Turn right after one mile, at the edge of a wood, keeping the trees on your left. Just before you reach Bowsers Farm, turn sharp left and follow the track straight ahead and over the gate at the bottom into a field. Go through the gate at the bottom left-hand corner of the field and head for another gate ahead of you. Through this, turn right on to the road, then turn right up the footpath by the side of the first  house on the right. Walk up the hill and through the farmyard, down the drive of Hall Farm and you will see Ashdon church and your car ahead of you.

Winster *to* Birchover   Approximately 4½ miles

*A hilly walk with
some short sharp
climbs, and some
superb rock scenery.*

Parking

OS Map 119 Ref 2460 In the
village of Winster along Main
Street.

Further Exploration

Winster

This is probably the best
surviving 18th-century mining
settlement in the Peak, most of
Main Street being of this age.
The 17th-century Market Hall is
now a National Trust Information
office.

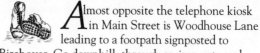 *A*lmost opposite the telephone kiosk in Main Street is Woodhouse Lane leading to a footpath signposted to Birchover. Go downhill, through an iron gate and soon a slabbed path bears left off the main track and along the hillside. The slabs disappear into a thick hedge so bear to the right of the hedge. At the bottom of the slope, take the left fork and climb steadily through a succession of three squeeze stiles, the final one being in the top left-hand corner of the field, near an electricity pole. This brings you to a minor road. Turn right and climb steeply up a narrow lane. Just over the brow of the hill, note a pair of stocks on the left-hand side. The village of Birchover now comes into view straight ahead on the hillside. On reaching the main street, turn left to the pub on the right.

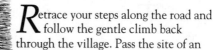 *R*etrace your steps along the road and follow the gentle climb back through the village. Pass the site of an ancient pinfold on the right, and opposite the quarry (Ann Twyfords), turn right onto a black surfaced track. After Bank Farm on the left, a stone squeeze stile brings you to a three-fingered signpost. Go straight ahead, bearing right for a gateway at the far side of the field, over a second field, to arrive at the top of a wooded valley. Follow the fence marking newly planted trees, and a more mature wood and, when clear of trees, go straight across the field to a hedge bordering a lane. Follow this stony lane downhill, and at a junction with the drive to Sabine Hey, turn right by Slough Wood. You eventually pass through a valley of spent overgrown mineral workings. The general direction is straight ahead, alongside a discoloured stream and through an area of overgrown undergrowth and trees. Cross the stream by a footbridge and head diagonally across the field to an isolated pair of stone uprights, and then to a stile clearly marked with a white painted pole. Cross a second complicated stile and head up to the road. Turn right towards Winster and your car.

Druid Inn (Free House)

This creeper-covered, 200-year-old pub beneath the Rowter Rocks, has one bar with several rooms, including a fairly modern extension. It is warmed by coal fires, the furniture is plain but comfortable, and the decor is traditionally simple. At the front of the building is a terrace with tables. Children are allowed in for meals, but not after 8pm. No dogs.

On draught: Mansfield, Marston Pedigree and Mild, Guinness, Fosters, Carlsberg, Strongbow cider. Food: A most extensive, international menu is shown on a blackboard. Large, scrumptious portions include chicken, ham and mushroom pie (£4.60), pork chops Tandoori-style (£5.20), tagliatelle (£3.80), and savoury nut loaf (£4.40). Puddings include Bakewell tart and brandy snap with fresh cream (both at £2.25). Food is served at 12-2 and 7-9pm. Tables may be booked in advance. Telephone: (062988) 302.

Parsley Hay *to* Hurdlow   Approximately 6 miles

A hilly walk with some marvellous views.

Parking

Map 119 Ref SK1265 Parsley Hay car park (High Peak Trail).

Further Exploration

Moneyash

Spare a few moments to admire the village with its old Market Cross, the 17th-century Hobbit Inn on the village green, St Leonard's Church and some picturesque cottages.

*L*eave Parsley Hay heading northwest and follow the old railway track. After crossing a bridge which goes over an unclassified road, you will soon arrive at the picnic area at Sparklow. Cross the road and continue on the trail under a road bridge. Immediately on your right, next to a trail sign, you will see a sunken footpath which leads to a kissing gate. From here, strike diagonally across the field to a dry-stone wall with a stile marked with a yellow footpath arrow. Continue uphill to reach the main road opposite the pub.

Bull i'th'Thorn (Robinson)

This is an old roadside farmhouse, first known as the Bull in 1472, then as the Hurdlow Thorn in the 17th-century. Today's title is a combination of the two. It stands high and solitary on the uplands beside the main A515. Over the main entrance is a carving depicting a bull caught in a thornbush and there are others, including an eagle with a freshly caught hare. Inside, the main bar is a Tudor hall full of oak beams, joists and panelling. Furnishings, too, are ancient, with carved and panelled seats, armour and swords on the thick walls, and an old flagstone floor. There is a large lawn with swings, and a family room.

On draught: Robinson Best and Mild, Guinness, Erinhorn, Strongbow cider. Food: Basic bar food includes ploughmans (from £2), steak and kidney pie (£2.75) and plaice (£2.50), both served with chips and peas. Full roasts are available at Sunday lunchtime. Food is served at 11.30-2pm and 6.45-9.30pm. Telephone: (029883) 348.

Arbor Low Stone Circle
This impressive monument from around 2000BC consists of three central and 47 perimeter stones. Relics have been found in an early Bronze Age barrow, including a stone cist containing a bone pin and two food vessels.

*T*ake the track to the left of the pub, descending between two dry-stone walls. Continue down this track and turn right at the bottom where the track passes some farm buildings on your left. Ignore the footpath sign No 3 on your left, but continue on the track to reach the road at Moneyash, bearing left here into the village. Turn right at the crossroads and continue along the road. This is a steep climb until you reach High Low Farm on your right. Continue on the road for about ¼ mile, watching out for some stone steps over the dry stone wall adjacent to an iron gate on your right – opposite a new farm house. Go straight across this field to another dry-stone wall, and on to the main A515 road. Almost immediately opposite, take another footpath leading down to the side of Moscar Farm. Cross the cattle grid on your right, turning immediately left through two iron gates, and continue down, crossing several stiles in dry stone walls to meet the High Peak Trail. Turn left here to return to Parsley Hay.

Youlgreave *to* Lathkill   Approximately 6 miles

A well-marked, though fairly demanding walk with some very rewarding views, taking you through a section of the Derbyshire Dales National Nature Reserve, where there is a diversity of flora and fauna to be found. Special care should always be taken in the vicinity of the mining remains.

Parking

OS Map 119 Ref SK9164 Car park at Moor Lane picnic site.

Further Exploration

Over Haddon is a beautiful hill-top village of limestone buildings, whose pretty church of St Anne is well worth a visit.

*A*t the bottom gate of the car park, turn right and walk past the picnic area, following the yellow 'Peak Park' arrow. Reaching a stile and gateway in the stone wall on your left, cross the stile and follow the footpath through a field, over two more stiles and down a hill to a road by an old limestone hut. Cross the stile into the road and bear left, following the 'Limestone Way' arrow. After a short distance, turn left into a field and take the public footpath to Over Haddon, following the yellow arrow marked with the number 1, over a stile, uphill, through a hole in the wall and past some farm buildings to a road. Cross over the road and continue to follow the yellow arrow across a field, a wall and along a path until you reach the next road. Go straight over the road into the opposite field (yellow arrows point left, do not follow them) and you will see the village of Over Haddon ahead. Walk towards the village, crossing two dry-stone walls (both marked with yellow arrows) and follow the public footpath up past Meadow Place Grange to your left, through the farmyard (public footpath sign) and several gates. Bear right across the next field and follow the footpath deep down into Lathkill Dale, then up the other side into the village. Walk through the main street to the end of the village and the pub.

Lathkill (Free House)

This busy and friendly pub has stunning views over the dale and over miles of beautiful Derbyshire countryside. There are low ceilings with oak beams, a small well kept bar with an open fireplace,.and a restaurant where children are welcome and which has a no smoking area.

On draught: Wards Sheffield Best, Darley Dark Mild, Darley Thorn Best, Tuborg. Food: There are generous portions of the homemade meals which include lasagne (£3.50), smoked trout fillet (£3.75), and lamb curry (£3.20), all served with chips and peas or a salad. For a smaller snack, try the cheese or meat cobs (rolls) with salad (from £1.35). Puddings include walnut flan, chocolate mousse and, of course, Bakewell tart. Food is served at 12-2pm and 7-9pm. Telephone: (0629) 812501.

*R*etrace your steps back to the bottom of the dale, and turn right through a gate at the house. Walk along the dale and through a second gate into the nature reserve. Follow the path along the river, through another gate and across an old wooden bridge (marked with yellow arrow number 2). Continue as far as a fork in the path, take the left fork downhill to a stile or the bottom of the hill, and then climb up the steep, stepped path on the other side. At the top, pass through the gate and head towards another gate through the field. After a third gate, follow the footpath up past some farm buildings on your right, and continue keeping the road to your right. At the corner of the field, head away from the road, over a stile and into a small copse. Out of the copse, follow the well-established footpath through the barleyfield, over a stile towards some road signs ahead. Cross another stile into the road and follow the signs to the picnic site car park.

Lathkill Dale Croft Centre in the village, has a number of individual workshops including stained glass, carpentry, lace-making, clock-making, and others. All workshops offer articles for sale. Open 10am - 5pm.

Lathkill Dale Lead Mining
A number of features from the Dale's past as a source of lead, remain and can be easily examined by the visitor, but do not attempt any underground exploration without expert guidance. The Peak District Mining Museum at Matlock Bath has extensive displays, public areas and information about lead mining in Derbyshire. Telephone: (0629) 583834.

Rowthorne *to* Hardwick Hall

Approximately 5 miles

An easy, straightforward walk, taking in a mixture of open arable farmland, woods and, for much of the way, parts of Hardwick Park surrounding Hardwick Hall. For some, the views will be spoilt by the sight of the M1.

Parking

OS Map 120 Ref 476647 Car park and picnic site just south of Rowthorne village.

Further Exploration

Hardwick Hall (National Trust) This spectacular Elizabethan house was built in 1591 for Bess of Hardwick, after the death of her fourth husband, the Earl of Shrewsbury. There are numerous tapestries with some fine needlework by Bess and her ladies, and by Mary, Queen of Scots who was the Earl of Shrewsbury's prisoner for 15 years. Walled courtyards enclose fine gardens. Telephone: (0246) 850430.

Turn right out of the car park and go up through the village. Just before The Old School on the right, take the footpath to the left. Go straight ahead, crossing two fields and a minor road. Head for a large gap with a lone tree on the far side and then for an obvious elbow in the road approaching Ault Hucknall. Immediately past the church, take the bridleway bearing off to the left. Pass a stone built house (1724) on the right and leave the track to pass through a gate on the left. Bear right down Broad Oak Hill, following a line of two stout posts, heading towards the distant water just coming into view. Cross another track and go through the gate in the fence opposite. Walk between two stretches of water, Millers Pond and Great Pond, to arrive at a small car park together with toilets and an information board relating to the Park. Backtrack for a short distance and take the path to the right with Great Pond ahead. Bear right, round the lake and head up towards the motorway. On reaching a road, turn left and left again following a signpost to Hardwick Hall. The pub is ahead of you on the right-hand side of the entrance to the Park.

Hardwick Inn (Free House)

A traditional, beautifully proportioned building of the early 17th century, set on the edge of Hardwick Park, has numerous original outbuildings and a large lawned garden. It contains two bars, two rooms where bar food is served, two family rooms, and a Carvery restaurant. It is warmed by coal fires, and is very comfortable and popular at all times. No dogs.

On draught: Younger's Scotch, Theakston XB, McEwan, Guinness, Autumn Gold and Dry Blackthorn ciders. Food: Homemade meals are mouthwatering, ample and moderately priced. Bar meals include T-bone steak (£7.50), scampi (£3.65), ploughmans (£2.50), and various vegetarian dishes (from £3.25). A children's menu is also available. In the Carvery (not Mondays), a choice of meats off the joint, plus a starter and sweet costs £7.75. Other main courses include 14oz T-bone steak (£11.25), and grilled trout (£7.75). Food is served at 11.30-2pm and 6.30-9.30pm. Advance booking is suggested for a table in the carvery. Telephone: (0246) 850245.

*T*urn right out of the pub and follow the road up the hill. At a sharp bend, leave the road and go through a gate on the right, cutting up to the left-hand corner of this field and a stile. At the top of a short incline, turn right and then almost immediately left into a wood. Through a gate out of the wood, turn left past Norwood Holiday Cottages. At Norwood Lodge, take the path to the left, walk along a private drive and straight across a field, aiming for a wood on the far side. Through the wood, cross a footbridge and stile, and in the next field, head for the left-hand corner. You are now on an old railway line and have a choice of paths back to your car. You can continue over the line and go straight ahead over four fields to reach a lane. Turn left here and left again at a road, to the car park. However, if this path is too muddy, turn left along the railway line and this will take you back to your car.

Bolsover Castle, Bolsover
Bess of Hardwick's son rebuilt this Norman castle in 1613. There are pseudo-Gothic vaulted ceilings, fine fireplaces, and ornate panelling. Be sure to see the elaborately painted ceilings of the 'star chamber', the Elysium room and the Heaven room. Telephone:(0246) 823349.

Higham, to the west, is a 17th century street village and a conservation area. Ogston reservoir is nearby.

Sherwood Forest and the Dukeries are to the east, including Clumber Park, Thoresby Park and Welbeck Abbey.

Grindon *to* Butterton   Approximately 6½ miles

This walk is not too arduous, although you must be prepared for lots of stiles and those narrow squeezes between stone slabs that are favoured in this area of stone walls. Superb views over the Manifold Valley and Dovedale to the hills of Derbyshire.

Parking

OS Map 119 SK0854 Grindon village church.

Further Exploration

The crags seen from the early part of this walk are above the Manifold Valley and its Thors Cave, both in reach of Grindon. That particular valley is well worth a visit, you could even hire cycles at Waterhouses on the A523 so that you could cover more distance.

Walk back towards the village but keep left past the church gate – you can cross the children's playground to achieve this. Descend the lane and turn left at the footpath sign. Continue down the field, over a brook, up into the next field, and over an unusual stile. Cross the road and another stile then descend by a well-defined path into the valley bottom to a sign which indicates you are at the base of Ossoms Hill. Cross the footbridge, over a stile and immediately turn left and over another stile into Hoo Brook Valley which you follow for a ¼ mile on its right side before crossing a stile and stepping stones to continue with the valley on its left side. At some cottages, cross a stile, then the brook again, and follow the road to the end, crossing a ford onto the footpath on the other side. Turn right up this path and cross footbridges to save getting wet feet, as this is both a road and stream bed. Climb up the quite steep hill and, shortly after passing the Manifold Arts and Craft Centre, bear right into a very narrow lane that will take you up to Butterton Church and the pub.

Black Lion Inn (Free House)

This welcoming, traditional village inn has a good reputation locally for both its food and beer. An ale house since 1782, it still retains a wealth of old beams and uneven floors that give it such character. There is a country dining room open on Friday and Saturday nights, and for Sunday lunch. Children are welcome.

On draught: Theakston Best, Younger's No 3, Scotch Bitter and Mild, Guinness, Becks, Taunton Blackthorn and Autumn Gold ciders. Food: Blackboard menus in the bars offer frequently changing items such as broccoli and cheese pie (£3.75), chicken curry or lasagne verdi (both £3.95), liver and onion, and ploughmans with four different cheeses (both £3). Food is served at 12-2pm and 7-9pm. Closed Wednesday lunchtime. Telephone: (05388) 232.

*T*urn left, then left again at the end of the car park, signposted to Onecote and Warslow. Just as the road starts to climb out of a dip, turn left onto a track and pass the front of Greenlow Head House, keeping left by the stone wall. Over a stile, walk through a narrow field and into another field which descends towards the valley bottom. Before you reach the corner of a wall, turn right towards a stile in a wall at the other side of the field. Keep on this clear footpath, through many stiles to a brook just beyond a tiny cottage. Keep to the right of the barn and head straight up the hill, past another farm, to the main road. Turn left and in about ¼ mile, turn right onto a track, immediately turning left and passing through a gate. Keep left, walk over a cattle grid, and at the next gate, turn left and continue alongside a fence, then a stone wall. Just after a long line of duckboards, climb over a stile then another on the right, and turn left alongside the wall to another stile. Keep to the left of the farm, and stiles will take you over the farm track, directly towards Grindon church, to the road. Cross, and follow the fingerpost over the next wall. The path is fairly obvious and heads back directly to Grindon church and your car.

Hanchurch Hills
to Swynnerton

Approximately 7 miles.

This is a pleasant walk through some dense forestry and rich arable land.

Parking

OS Sheet 127 SJ8339
Hanchurch Hills Picnic Site

Further Exploration

Swynnerton is a delightful village dominated by the 17th-century manor house. Swynnerton Park encloses almost the whole village with its copses, woods, arable and pasture land. There are many buildings of interest, including the 12th-century Church of St. Mary, the Victorian 'Tudor' school, an 18th-century rectory and numerous thatched cottages. It is also believed that Swynnerton was the inspiration for Longfellow's *Under the Spreading Chestnut Tree* and you will see one as you step out of the Fitzherbert Arms.

*B*eyond the County Council map of the area in its glass case, you will see a finger post which you head for and turn right onto the track which descends into the wood. At the bottom, go through the gate and turn left onto the road. In barely ½ mile, turn left through gate onto a wide track. Keep right and gently descend through the farm then, at a T-junction, turn right towards the lovely red and yellow brick water pumping works at Hatton. At the main road, turn right passing the entrance to the water works then almost immediately turn left. After a short distance, turn left onto a track passing a farm then, in about ½ mile, just after passing a remote little cottage, turn left through a gate. The path is clearly marked and soon crosses a main road. At the top of the second field, the path kinks through the hedge and continues on the other side, to a wide farm track and a T-junction. Cross over to the waymarked path between hedges and bracken which will take you into the village of Swynnerton. Keep straight along the lane to the pub.

Fitzherbert Arms (Bass)

This is a comfortable looking, dark brick inn that is believed to have been a farm originally. Recently refurbished, there are lots of cosy sitting areas and a restaurant for meals by arrangement (generally only open at weekends).

On draught: Bass Draught and Mild, Worthington, Guinness, Carling Black Label, Tennents Pilsner and Extra, Dry Blackthorn cider. Food: Hot and cold meals range from ploughmans (£3.75), curry (£2.60), haddock (£3.80), homemade steak and kidney pie (£3.50) or Fitzherbert pie, using various meats and vegetables. There is also a good range of sandwiches including the Fitzherbert 'Special', a chicken triple-decker (£3). Telephone: (078135) 542.

*F*rom the front of the pub, turn left, then left again by SP Beech. Pass another red and yellow brick water tower to the main road, turn right then immediately left onto a wide vehicular track. At far end, bear right down the hill then left just before the gate to the tiny hamlet of Beech. At the fork, bear right by the concrete and metal railings and down the hill. Join another road to climb up the hill and pass under a narrow arch bridge, shortly turning right, then at a T-junction, turn left. At a fork by a farm gate, bear right and this pot-holed road will take you back to the tall water tower and your car. If you prefer a more natural path, bear right shortly after the farm gate and enter the wood, a path runs parallel to the road, just keep to the top of the wood and do not descend.

The most dominant features of the walk are the Grade II listed Italianate yellow and red brick water works at Hatton and the water towers at Hanchurch and Swynnerton. For a glimpse of steam-driven power, Mill Meece Pumping Station is open to the public at weekends.

Parkgate *to* Lower Peover   Approximately 6 miles

A pleasant walk through Cheshire's fields and lanes, crossing the landscaped grounds of Peover Hall.

Parking
OS Map 118 Ref SJ7874
Outside Parkgate village hall.

Further Exploration
St Oswald's Church, Lower Peover
This church dates largely from the Tudor period, and is a black and white timbered building with a stone tower, famous for its ancient and massive oak dug-out chest. Local tradition says that any girl aspiring to be a Cheshire farmer's wife had to be strong enough to fling back the lid with one hand.

Jodrell Bank Radio Telescope is at the nearby village of Goostrey and the Science Centre is open to visitors most days.
Telephone: (0477) 71339.

Head away from the post office, up the lane past some cottages on your right, and then left into the parkland of Peover Hall, taking a broad tree-lined grassy avenue. At the end of this, cross the stile into a meadow, and continue straight ahead to the opposite side and a stile, just to the right of the Peover Hall. Cross into the lane and turn left to come to another lane. Sharp right is a path back into the park to St Lawrence's Church (locked) but take the next right along a quiet lane skirting the park, presently passing St Anthony's cottages. Continue through a gate onto a bridleway. (If you decide to see the church, keep the churchyard on your right, go under a pleached arch of trees, follow the path through woodland to a stile, cross the neck of the field, over another stile and turn left to follow a track past the end of a row of cottages and on to join the bridleway). Follow the bridleway to the A50. Cross the main road into Free Green Lane, and follow this before turning left by some cottages. Turn right at the T-junction, continuing to another by Well Cottage. Turn left on to Free Green Lane again, continue to a post office (looking just like a private house) and turn left, then left again down a cul-de-sac that crosses a stream and brings you to Lower Peover church and the pub.

Bells of Peover (Greenhall Whitney)

 The white-painted walls of this charming old pub are covered with wisteria and there are tables on the patio in summer. Inside is a series of attractive, traditionally furnished rooms, some small, some large, with a fine collection of Toby jugs. Children under 14 are not allowed in the bar, though welcome at the tables outside or in the restaurant.

On draught: Greenhall Whitney Bitter and Mild, Guinness, guest beers, Grünhalle, Export Gold, Labatt's, and a good selection of wines. Food: Meals range from steak and kidney pie (£3.60) or roast chicken (£3.75) to filled potatoes (from £2.75) and a variety of sandwiches (from £1.20). Food is served at 12-2pm and 6.30-8.30pm. There is a separate restaurant open Tuesday - Friday, Saturday evening (7-9.30pm) and Sunday lunchtime. Telephone: (0565) 722269.

*R*etrace your steps to Free Green Lane, turn right and continue straight on past the Well Cottage turning until you come to Free Green Farm (just before you come to an old black and white cottage on the right of the lane). Turn left down the farm drive and keep left through the farmyard to find a long, straight bridleway which leads you, eventually, past a farm to the A50. Cross the road and turn right to reach a Gothic lodge cottage beside the Whipping Stocks pub. To the right of the cottage, a drive leads through the wooded parkland of Peover Hall, passing the edge of the lake and leading straight up to the Hall gates. Go through the edge of the garden to join the lane where the stile into the meadow allows you to retrace your steps to Parkgate. As an alternative to entering the garden, you can either skirt the garden wall on the meadow side to pick up the footpath or, as you approach the Hall and the church, you could veer right to the stile into the wood to join the path leading back past the church, and so retrace your steps to Parkgate.

Bickley Moss *to* Cholmondeley

Approximately 6 miles

A walk on quiet country lanes through the pastoral landscape of the Cheshire plain near Cholmondeley Castle.

Parking
OS Map 117 Ref SJ5349 Near the church.

Further Exploration
Cholmondeley Castle
The grounds and gardens, immediately opposite the pub on the other side of the main road, are open from Easter to September on Sundays and Bank Holidays. Telephone: (0829) 720383.

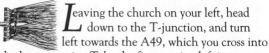

*L*eaving the church on your left, head down to the T-junction, and turn left towards the A49, which you cross into the lane opposite. Take the first turning left into a lane that winds past Norbury Common to a crossroads. Here, turn left and continue to another crossroads, turning left again. At Chorley Bank, a sharp left-hand bend brings you to what looks like a village school, standing on your right, a little way back from the corner with the main road.

Cholmondeley Arms (Marston)

This most unusual pub was a village school until 1982 and only became a pub in 1988. The interior retains its character, the large, high-ceilinged, interconnecting school rooms forming a T-shape with the bar at the centre and a gallery above.

On draught: Marston Pedigree, Burton Best, Carlsberg, Hofmeister, Stella Artois, Heineken, Guinness, Strongbow. There is also a guest beer. Food: There is a large range of imaginative specials displayed on a blackboard. Braised beef with ginger, salmon and spinach lasagne, crisply fried whitebait, home-made soups, ploughmans, salads and sandwiches are among the choices, and prices for main dishes range from £3-£7. There is also a children's menu. Telephone: (0829) 720300.

*T*urn right out of the yard to come to the A49, and cross over into the lane skirting the beautiful wooded grounds of Cholmondeley Castle. You will pass a track on the left leading to Red Hall, but continue to the next turning on your left and follow this lane down, going straight over the crossroads until you come to a T-junction where a left turn brings you back to Bickley Church.

Approximately 5 miles

Keld *to* Muker

 alk into the small square and take the arrowed footpath in the north-east corner. At a junction of paths, keep straight on, pass through a gate and climb uphill. Follow the Pennine Way signs up to a gap in a wall and along the edge of Kisdon Hill. Cross numerous wall stiles eventually going downhill towards a derelict house. Leave the Pennine Way here and follow a steep lane downhill into the village of Muker.

This is a delightful ramble through Upper Swaledale affording views of upland moorland and the green fields of the Swale valley.

Parking
OS Map 92 Ref NY8901. Keld village.

Farmers Arms (Free House)

 Set back from the road, this welcoming white-painted pub is truly a farmer's local. The bar is L-shaped, and has comfortable cushioned wall- seats and pine tables. There are a few prints hanging on the walls, and a small shelf near the entrance offers visitors some reading books and leaflets on local places of interest. Outside, the front terrace has good bench seating with views up into fields. Children are welcome.

On draught: John Smithshire, Youngers, Theakston Old Peculiar and XB, Fosters, Carlsberg. Food: Good value food includes filled baps (£1), toasted sandwiches (£1.15), omelettes (£2.75), lasagne (£2.75), jacket potato with cheese (£1.20) and soup (£1). Food is served at 12-2pm and 7-9pm. Telephone: (0748) 86297.

Further Exploration
Muker is the largest of a trio of delightful villages near the head of Swaledale. Situated at the foot of Kisdon Hill are grey stone cottages, an Elizabethan church, a chapel and an Institute – all village additions during the lead-mining days, remains of which are evident on the hillside. Pioneer botanists Cherry and Richard Kearton, who were the first to use photographs for illustrating botanical books, went to school here and are commemorated in the chapel. The Pennine Way, coming in from Kisdon Hill and part of this walk, follows the old 'Corpse Way'. This was the route coffin-bearers used from Muker to the church at Grinton, before the church at Muker was built.

*B*ack through the village, follow the footpath waymarked to Keld and Gunnerside. Through a stile, follow the established path across meadowland. Cross a footbridge over the River Swale, bear left and follow the track along the river. After a mile, at Swinner Gill, pass through a gate and climb the steep track which leads up to the remains of Crackpot Hall – a short diversion to the right. Keep to the path, then in a short distance, fork left downhill passing East Gill Force on the left, and cross a wooden bridge over the Swale. Follow the path uphill to join your outward route back to Keld square.

Askrigg *to* Bainbridge

Approximately 5 miles

A beautiful walk affording panoramic views across the length of Wensleydale and beyond to the austere moorland.

Parking

OS Map 98 Ref SD9491 Near the village church.

Further Exploration

Askrigg

This is an interesting stone village in the heart of Wensleydale with most of the buildings being of the 18th and 19th centuries, arising from Askrigg's increasing prosperity through its clock-making, lead-mining and textiles. Today, the village bustles with tourists, for it is famous as a location for the filming of *All Creatures Great and Small*. James Herriot country includes Wensleydale and Swaledale, where his vetinary practice was concentrated. The whole area is full of associations with the real life James Herriot and the locations for filming.

*F*ollow the signs to Mill Gill Force, starting at the lane beside the church wall heading west out of village, past several houses, along a waymarked path, across a field, and uphill through the edge of woodland. At a junction of paths, continue straight on (or bear right to see a waterfall), eventually taking a footpath on the left over a stile waymarked to Helm. Cross two fields to a lane, bear left then immediately right, and follow the very quiet lane towards Skelgill. Cross a narrow bridge and take the footpath over a stile down beside a narrow beck. Keep to this path across fields and a stile, eventually heading downhill to a lane. Bear left and cross the lane, following a footpath down across the course of an old railway, to a road and a bridge. Follow this road into Bainbridge, and the pub is on the right side of the green.

Rose and Crown (Free House)

One of the finest of the handsome old buildings that skirt the village green, this is a splendid 15th-century coaching inn. The famous Bainbridge horn, traditionally blown to guide lost travellers, stands in the entrance hall, beyond which are a mellow bar, a cosy little snug and a very comfortable lounge with log stove. The beamed and panelled front bar has antique settles and other old furniture, a butterfly collection and a splendid open fire. There are excellent views out across the green from the windows. Children are welcome.

On draught: Theakston, John Smith, Younger's Scotch, Guinness, Fosters, Carlsberg. Food: Good substantial bar food includes ploughmans (£3.50), lamb casserole (£4.85), sandwiches (from £1.65), Bedale ham and eggs (£4.85), and local sausage and baked potato (£3.95). Food is served at 12-2 and 6-8.30pm (from 7pm in the restaurant. Telephone: (0969) 50225.

Walk along the edge of the green following the main road, cross the bridge over the river, pass the petrol station and, at a road junction, bear right onto a lane and take the waymarked path on the left. Follow this uphill across fields and stiles, eventually walking along the top of a ridge. Entering the edge of woodland on top of a crag, take the footpath downhill to a stile. Cross, and follow the waymarked path across the field diagonally to the right, down towards the corner and the hamlet of Worton. Pass through two gates, bear right then left on the road through Worton. Eventually cross a bridge and take path signposted to Askrigg across meadowland, entering the village along a narrow lane, back to the church and car.

Glaisdale *to* Egton Bridge

Approximately 5 miles

Not a long walk but a fairly robust one with some short bursts of lung-stretching climbing through the delightful wooded Esk Valley.

Parking

OS Map 94 Ref NZ7705. Underneath the railway arches by Glaisdale Station.

Further Exploration

Glaisdale

One of the bridges which span the River Esk is the tiny Beggars Bridge, built in 1619 by Tom Ferris, a local boy made good, as a gesture to prove his worth to the doubting father of the Egton girl he courted.

*T*he road climbs up from the railway to Glaisdale village. To your left is a track marked 'Unsuitable for Motors'. Turn up here, ignoring the footpath signposted to Arncliffe Wood. The stoney track climbs steeply uphill to the left passing a cottage on your right. When the main track carries on through a gate, follow the clear path that veers off, still steeply, to the left. As the incline lessens, ignore the footpath to the left which goes over a wooden stile wall, but bear right and keep climbing steadily. After about ¼ mile, a National Park footpath sign marks a clear track to your left. Follow the sign through the gate along the track until you reach the unclassified road from Rosedale to Egton Bridge. Turn left and follow the road downhill for about ¾ mile to the ford where salmon can be seen crossing the road when the river is running high. Round the corner from the ford is the pub.

Horseshoe Inn (Free House)

Picturesquely situated on the banks of the River Esk, this charming pub has a large and well-kept garden with plenty of tables for outdoor drinking and eating. It even has its own island in the middle of the River Esk, which is sometimes open to the public. Inside there is an unspoilt, comfortable 'L'-shaped bar, in part of which children are allowed. Like all pubs in this beautiful area, it gets very busy in the summer but service is always brisk and efficient.

On draught: Theakston, Tetley, Castlemaine XXXX, Carlsberg. Food: Good quality home cooked meals are served in generous portions, Yorkshire style. Typical dishes include steak and kidney pie (£4.20), steak (£7) and freshly cut sandwiches (from £1.50). There is also a separate restaurant with an à la carte menu. Food is served at 12-2pm and 6-9pm. Telephone: (0947) 85245.

Egton Bridge
This is one of England's most famous Roman Catholic parishes, known as 'the village missed by the Reformation'. It is the birthplace of Father Nicholas Postgate, 'Martyr of the Moors' who kept the faith alive when Roman Catholics were persecuted. He was executed in York, aged 82, for baptising a child into the Catholic faith in 1679.

Walk up the left-hand drive to the road and then immediately turn left down the short path that leads to the River Esk. Cross the two sets of stepping stones and follow the path onto the road which runs on the far bank of the river. At the road, turn left and follow the road and river under the railway bridge, up the hill, to a footpath sign on your left pointing over a stile. Follow this path, keeping the fence to your left, to the beck where there is a footpath sign on a tree. Cross the field as indicated up a very steep, but mercifully short slope and cross the stile at the end of the conifer wood. Follow the steep path through the wood and over another stile, keeping the hedge to your left at all times. Over the next stile, follow the track past the television mast, and you will see a farmyard in front of you. Do not follow the path right through the farmyard, but veer left by the water-trough to the gate, and then turn right onto the road. This is Limber Hill. Turn left and follow the road as it drops down to the River Esk again and then back to the railway arches at Glaisdale.

Malham Tarn *to* Malham   Approximately 6 miles

A beautiful walk through some of the finest limestone scenery in Britain. The view from the top of the Cove is magnificent – a panorama down the Aire valley into the southern dales. Take care on the loose stones which can be especially nasty when wet.

Parking
OS Map 98 Ref SD8965
Malham Tarn car park.

Further Exploration
Malham Tarn
This is 1km across but only 5 metres deep at the most. It is unique in Britain in being the only upland lime-rich lake of any significant size. Generally, water will sink through the porous limestone but the tarn is on slate, which is impermeable, and is surrounded by limestone rocks which give it its lime-rich character. It is a haven for lime-loving plants and wintering duck.

*T*urn left from the car park onto the road and cross a stream, taking the path on the left (waymarked) through a gate. Follow this grassy path, keeping left, heading downstream until you reach a fork in the path. Bear left towards Water Sinks and Malham Cove on the path winding downhill, eventually bearing left over a stile and down the middle of the Watlowes valley. When the path bears right onto the rock 'pavement' on top of Malham Cove, cross the pavement (with care), climb over a ladder stile, descend the steps into the cove, and follow the stream to the foot of the cove wall. Follow this established path to a road. Bear left and remain on this road into the village of Malham. To find the pub, turn left over the bridge.

Lister Arms (Free House)

This large stone pub sits in a beautiful location, close to the stream which flows through the village. Inside, the main bar is warm and welcoming with two open fires burning in large stone fireplaces. There is plenty of comfortable seating in the carpeted bar, and a second room houses a pool table. There is also a garden with tables should you wish to eat outside.

On draught: Younger's Scotch, Henry Wadworth IPA, Burton Ale, Moorhouse's Pendle Witches Brew, Guinness. Food: Blackboard lunchtime menu offers good hearty meals including steak and Guinness pie (£3.75), ham and courgette bake (£3.50), sandwiches from (£1.40) and ploughmans (£3.20). There is also a separate children's menu. Food is served at 12-2pm and 7.30-9pm (9.30pm in the restaurant). No food is served on Mondays, and it is essential to book on Saturday evenings. Telephone: (07293) 330.

R eturn across the bridge and bear left, shortly to cross back over the stream, and take the path over a stile, waymarked 'Pennine Way', following Malham Beck downstream. At the third stile, take the path following the wall on the left away from the Pennine Way towards a barn. Keep to the footpath, crossing a stile, now following Gordale Beck. Enter the National Trust woodland, and the path eventually reaches Janet's Foss – a small 16ft high waterfall. Legend has it that the cave it guards was the home of Jenet, the queen of the local fairies. When the path joins a lane, bear right and walk to Gordale Bridge. Take the path arrowed 'Malham Cove' on the right and look out for the fields to the left which contain signs of several Iron Age hut circles and enclosures. Follow the yellow markers uphill through gates and over stiles until you eventually reach a lane. Turn left and follow the lane uphill for ½ mile before crossing a stile and following the path arrowed to the left. Follow this grassy path across the scarred limestone landscape and moorland. Keep bearing left and join the Pennine Way, cross a stile and return to the road and the car park.

Malham Cove
One of England's great natural wonders, with its 70 metre high sheer walls. Formed by the combined erosional effects of both ice and water on the weak Craven Fault. Twelve thousand years ago, meltwater would have flowed down the Watlowes valley, then over the cliff as a waterfall. Glaciers, too, flowed over the cliff at some stage. The result is the beautiful, yet striking wide cove with Malham Beck now flowing out from the base of the cliff.

Before reaching the path to Water Sinks and Malham Cove at the beginning of your walk, on your right about 1km away is a chimney which is the remains of a smelt mill used in the 19th century to smelt local lead, ore and zinc ore.

A good diversion from the main route is to follow the path waymarked to Gordale Scar. Follow the stream into a gorge where the walls are only 15 metres apart. It is a beautiful, dramatic gorge formed by powerful glacial meltwater carving its way down a weakness or fault in the rock. The magnificent double waterfall cascades through a window in the rock, but when it is not in spate, it may be climbed with care.

Flasby *to* Hetton

Approximately 4 miles

A peaceful ramble along Eshton Beck and the moorland flanks of Flasby Fell.

Parking
OS Ref SD9456 Map 103.
Hamlet of Flasby

Head downhill towards a farm and take the path on the left waymarked to Hetton. Follow the path along the banks of the small Eshton Beck, across stiles and fields. When you see fingerposts to Hetton pointing away from the beck, follow these across fields to join a road, and bear right into the village of Hetton. The pub lies on left at the far end of village.

Angel (Free House)

This elegant stone pub has four tastefully decorated rooms with some beams, standing timbers, comfortable wall-settle seating and country kitchen chairs. A warm welcome awaits, especially in winter – there are log fires, a solid-fuel stove and the main bar has a farmhouse range in its stone fireplace. Attractive pictures and sepia photographs adorn the walls, and fresh flowers add a splash of colour. At the front of the pub, wooden benches and tables are set out on the cobbles. Children are welcome in the eating area and restaurant.

On draught: Theakston Bitter and XB, Taylor Landlord, Tetley, Guinness, Carlsberg, Beck's. There is also a good wine list. Food: Meals are imaginatively presented and good value for money. The menu includes Provençale fish soup (£1.95), local goat's cheese baked in filo pastry, with French leaves dressed in walnut vinaigrette (£3.85), ragout of venison (£5.75), salmon with cucumber and dill (£5.95), and spinach noodles with garlic and basil sauce (£3.45). Sandwiches (from £1.95) are available at lunchtime. Puddings include creme brûlée and summer pudding (from £2.15). Food is served at 12-2pm (2.30pm on Sunday) and 6-10pm (not Sunday). Telephone: (075673) 263.

*R*eturn back along the road as far as the footpath on the left, signposted to Rylstone. Follow this to a house on the left with a large picture window, and take the wall stile on the right, crossing a field and passing through two gates to cross the railway. Head towards and pass behind a barn, passing through another gate on the right. Continue straight on through a further two gates, and cross the field to a stone stile. Over the stile, bear diagonally left across the field and follow the track under the railway, heading towards a stone wall. Cross the ladder stile and go directly uphill to a gate into a small copse and on towards another gate. Through this, head down to a farm, following the signs to Flasby. After the farm, bear right off the track, through a gate and across the meadow to another gate and a fingerpost. Follow this footpath downhill into the farmyard and on to Flasby.

Barden Bridge *to* Appletreewick

Approximately 5½ miles

A beautiful and peaceful walk along the River Wharf with outstanding valley scenery. Birds to look out for include herons and kestrels, dippers and wagtails.

Parking

OS Maps 98,99 & 104 Ref SE0557 Parking area near Bardon Bridge.

Further Exploration

Barden Tower
Located over the gracefully arched Bardon Bridge and uphill on the B-road, this tower is a ruined three-storey hunting lodge which overlooks the River Wharf.

Bolton Abbey
One of England's more romantic abbey ruins and parkland on the banks of the river, is just three miles south of the Bardon Bridge. The abbey was founded by Augustinian canons in 1151 and the nave is complete and now used as a parish church.

Parcevall Hall Gardens, Skyreholme near Appletreewick
In a beautiful hillside setting, east of the main Wharfdale valley, the gardens of this Elizabethan house are open daily. Telephone: (075672) 311.

*F*ollow the lane away from the bridge for a short distance before taking footpath signposted to Howgill Inn.   This well-established path, the Dales Way, follows the river Wharf upstream for nearly two miles. Soon after a short stretch of woodland beside a small waterfall, there is a campsite beside the river, and here you bear right onto the path signposted to Appletreewick. When you join a road, turn right and follow uphill to the pub.

Craven Arms (Free House)

This fine pub has two small and intimate bars with open fires, and one even has an old black kitchen range.   Beamed ceilings, stone walls, attractive settles and carved chairs combine to create a cosy and welcoming atmosphere. Hundreds of bank notes adorn the ceiling, while old agricultural tools, copper pans and brassware are dotted around the rooms. Outside, there are plenty of bench seats on which to admire the outstanding views. Children are welcome.

On draught: Theakston Best and XB, Tetley, Younger's Scotch, Guinness. Food: Generous portions of good value meals include vegetable and pasta bake (£3.20), steak and kidney pie (£3.25), and local pork sausage, jacket potato and salad (£2.95). Food is served at 12-2pm and 7-9pm(or 9.30pm at weekends). Telephone: (075672) 270.

*F*ollow the lane through Appletreewick and take the second turning right towards Skyreholme. In a short distance, take the waymarked footpath on your right through a farmyard, and bear right through a gate. Pass a campsite on the left and cross a stile, following a path downhill to join a lane. Bear left, cross a bridge and rejoin the Dales Way along the river bank back to Barden Bridge.

Buckden *to* Hubberholme

Walk down to a small green by the post office. Cross the green and follow a lane over a bridge, then take the footpath (Dales Way) on the right and follow the path beside the River Wharfe, signposted to Hubberholme. Follow this path to a lane, then turn right into the quiet hamlet of Hubberholme. The pub is on the left by the bridge.

George Inn (Free House)

This remote and unspoilt pub in a peaceful hamlet offers a relaxing break and a friendly welcome. The bar is quite small and has burnished copper-topped tables, stone walls, flagstone floors, beams and a large warming fireplace with a wood-burning stove. A second bar also offers comfortable seating and has stone walls adorned with numerous prints. Good seating on the terrace catches the sun and faces the moors. Children are welcome in the room next to the bar.

On draught: Younger's No 3 and Scotch, Harp, Beck's. Food: A small menu offers good value, hearty food and includes large baps filled with choice of cheese, ham, tuna or beef (£2), homemade soup (£1.20), steak and kidney pie (£3.75), turkey, ham and chicken pie (£3.75) and ploughmans (£2.30). Food is served at 12-2pm & 7-9pm. Telephone: (075676) 223.

Cross the bridge towards the church and take the footpath adjacent to the churchyard waymarked 'Scargill & Yockenthwaite' and follow this uphill. Pass behind Scar House and, at a fingerpost, take the path waymarked to Cray, along the edge of the wood. Keep following yellow markers on rocks and posts and pass through farmyard down into Cray. Cross the road and stream near the White Lion and follow the path uphill waymarked 'Buckden'. Keep to this track through fields and gates below Buckden Pike to the car park.

An idyllic ramble along lush meadowland paths and upland tracks affording panoramic views of upper Wharfdales glacial valley and hillsides and of Langstrothdale. Look out for river birds, namely the dipper and grey wagtails.

Parking
OS Map 98 Ref SD9477
Buckden car park.

Further Exploration
Hubberholme
Of particular interest is its church 'St Michael & all Angels' which originated as a forest chapel. It is probably the best-loved of all Dales churches, with its superb riverside setting against a backcloth of wooded hillside and distant bare fells. It is noted for its broad, low profile and short tower and inside for its woodwork. The work of Robert Thompson can be identified by his 'signature' – delightful carved mice on the pews and in other unusual places. The ashes of the author J.B. Priestley, are scattered nearby and a plaque is dedicated to him in the church.

Pateley Bridge *to* Wath in Nidderdale

Approximately 5½ miles

This is a tranquil river walk through beautiful Nidderdale with a return route affording panoramic views of the dale and surrounding hills and moors.

Parking

OS Map 99 Ref SE1565. Car park in centre of Pateley Bridge.

Further Exploration

Pateley Bridge and Nidderdale
This was once the most industrialised of the major Yorkshire dales, based on flax-growing and the manufacture of linen and hemp and relying on water power from the river and its tributaries. When steam-powered mills mechanised the textile industry, linen manufacture decreased and Pateley's mills turned to making cord, twine and rope along, with quarrying and mining. Now however, prosperity is found in agriculture and tourism. The history of Nidderdale can be traced by visiting the fascinating Nidderdale Museum, once a Victorian workhouse, which illustrates all aspects of the past. Telephone: (0473) 71125.

*T*ake the footpath waymarked 'Wath' on the town side of the river, and head upstream. Follow a sign pointing around the back of some houses, eventually reaching the river bank. The path runs parallel to the River Nidder across meadowland, close to, and occasionally along the course of the old railway line. Follow this path up to a quiet lane and narrow humped-back bridge, turning right and following the lane to the pub.

*R*eturn along the lane and cross the bridge. At a T-junction, cross and take the path waymarked to Heathfield and continue uphill across fields and stiles, guided by green signs with yellow arrows. Pass behind Spring Hill Farm and bear right at a quiet lane into the tiny hamlet of Heathfield. In a short distance, turn left along a track waymarked to Mosscar. Follow uphill and at the top, follow the 'Nidderdale Way' sign through a gate into a field. Keep to the hedge and follow the path through some gates, keeping the stone building to the left, and eventually bear right passing through two black gates at a farm. Walk downhill across the field, keeping to the stone wall, to a quiet lane. Bear left, then right through a gate – signposted to Nidderdale Way – passing beside a caravan site. Cross the stream, follow the track uphill, then keep left to follow a path between two stone walls, heading towards a house. Cross the brook and follow a sign and path passing in front of the house and remain on the track until you join a road. Bear left, passing the Wheel Inn – once an old flax mill, whose huge mill wheel has been renovated and is still working – and in short distance, take the path on the right signposted to Pateley Bridge. Cross the meadows on the established path to join the river bank and walk back to the town and car park.

Sportsman's Arms (Free House)

This is an old sandstone coaching inn, set back from the road, with a well-kept garden prettily decorated with hanging flower baskets. The inn is split into lounge, dining room and bar. The comfortable, panelled bar is reached from the side of the pub and is modern in decor with chintzy fabrics, carpet and smart tables. Quality prints adorn the wall. The welcome is warm and friendly to both adults and children.

On draught: Younger's Scotch, McEwan's Export, Guinness, Harp, Beck's. Food: Good quality bar lunches are available with emphasis being on fish dishes – fresh from Whitby or the local Nidderdale trout. Meals are imaginatively presented with good salads. The menu includes homemade soup (£1.80), locally made and Continental cheese with pickles, wholemeal bread and salad (£3.20), Nidderdale trout (£5), Spanish omelette (£4.50), french baguette with chicken Waldorf (£4.20). Desserts include lemon torte and passion cake. Bar food is served at 12-2 only. Telephone: (0423) 711306.

Kilburn *to* Coxwold

Approximately 4½ miles

A gentle, undemanding walk largely through rolling farm land, with fine views of the escarpment from which the notorious Sutton Bank descends.

Parking

OS Map 100 Ref SE5180
Middle of the village by the
Foresters Arms.

Further Exploration

Kilburn

As well as being an attractive village in its own right, Kilburn is well-known for its famous White Horse carved into the hillside above the village in 1857 by the headmaster of the village school, assisted by his conscripted pupils and village volunteers. It is visible for miles around and particularly so on this walk.

Kilburn is also renowned as the home of its most favourite craftsmen, Robert Thompson, a woodcarver whose furniture can be found all over the world and whose hallmark was, and still is, a small mouse which always decorates any piece of furniture or carving made by him or his successors. He died in 1955 but his grandsons have carried on the family tradition. His old home in the main village street is now a showroom for the firm's work and is open to the public.

Walk south through the village past a number of attractive cottages until about a ¼ mile out of the village you will reach a large, rather incongruous, modern factory building. Turn left opposite this, along a footpath which becomes a little indistinct. After crossing several fields, you will reach a track which, if you turn left, goes back into Kilburn. Turn right, heading behind the attractive barns. After passing the barns on your right, the footpath turns sharp left and follows a line of trees. Just beyond a water-trough at the end of the field, there is a stile which you cross and turn right along the hedged path to a narrow lane. Turn right here along the lane past Kilburn Thicket – rich with young pheasants and other game bird – and Fox Folly Farm. The lane soon joins the road back to Kilburn. Opposite the right-hand turn, proceed through a white gate and bear right across the field to another white gate which brings you out almost next to Shandy Hall. The pub lies just beyond this on the left-hand side of the village street.

Turn left out of the pub and, almost immediately, there is a footpath running off the main street down to the fields behind the village. Follow this, turning left after a short distance. The path then runs diagonally to your left across the fields. After approximately ½ mile, there is a footpath to your left which you follow to the road just south of Fox Folly Farm. Proceed along the road for a short distance, taking the signposted bridleway across the fields to your left, which brings you out onto the Kilburn Road by the entrance drive to Wildon Grange. Turn right along the Kilburn Road back to the village.

Fauconberg Arms (Free House)

 This seventeenth century inn is named after the Earl of Fauconberg who lived at nearby Newburgh Hall and was married to Cromwell's daughter, Mary. There is a belief that Mary brought her father's body to the Hall after his death in 1658 and that it lies undiscovered in a bricked-up vault. The current landlord and his wife have run this charming pub for nearly a quarter of a century. There is a comfortable lounge and a bright, cheerful public bar with stone walls, huge beams, flagstone floors and a great fireplace. Children are tolerated.

On draught: Theakston Best, Tetley, Younger's Scotch, Guinness, Carlsberg. There is also and extensive wine list and no less than 10 champagnes for the more well-heeled tourist. Food: Bar food is usually limited to sandwiches (£1.50) and soup (£1.50) and served at 12-1.30pm. No bar food is available on Sundays or in the evening, but the pub's restaurant serves traditional food each evening 7-9pm. Telephone: (03476) 214.

Shandy Hall
This attractive house was the home of Laurence Sterne, vicar of Coxwold in the 18th century and author of *The Life and Opinions of Tristram Shandy, Gentlemen.* Shandy Hall itself dates from the 15th and 17th centuries. It contains the largest collection anywhere of Sterne's books and manuscripts and other Sterne memorabilia. It is also open to the public. Telephone: (03476) 465.

Hutton le Hole *to* Lastingham

Approximately 5 miles

A gentle, undulating walk on the southern edge of the North Yorkshire Moors, taking in two of the area's most attractive villages.

Parking

OS Map 100 Ref SE7090 Public car park at the north end of the village.

Further Exploration

Hutton le Hole
This has claims to be one of the most photographed villages in the North Yorkshire Moors and its attractiveness cannot be denied, although sometimes, the sheer volume of tourists can detract from it. Like many parts of the National Park, it is best appreciated out or season.

Ryedale Folk Museum
Opened in 1964, this museum conveys a realistic impression of rural life in the area over the last four centuries. An interesting feature is the way in which whole cottages have been removed from neighbouring villages and rebuilt on site. Telephone: (07515) 367.

Walk south down the main village street, past the Ryedale Folk Museum, until you come to a gate on your left with a footpath sign. Follow the path past the bowling green and cross the stile. Follow the fence on your left, ignoring the next stile on the left, and proceed to the corner of the field and cross the stile. Keeping the fence to your left, pass through a gate, cross the stream and follow the footpath through the wood. This brings you out onto the minor road from Hutton le Hole to Lastingham with the North Yorkshire Moors starting to rise on your left. Turn right, following the path along the grass verge. Just before the bridge over the beck, turn left over a stile and follow the path along the Moor edge to Camomile Farm. Do not go through the farmyard, but bear left, and follow the wall on your right where it turns a corner. The path goes across the beck and rises to a seat overlooking Lastingham village. Turn right at the seat, down the path into the village, and the pub is opposite the church.

Blacksmiths Arms (Free House)

This is an attractive, welcoming pub with a number of small traditionally furnished rooms. It is slightly unusual for the area in that it utilises the recently granted right to remain open all day, even in the off season. There are a few seats and tables outside the pub and a small and secluded beer garden at the back.

On draught: Wilson, Websters, Ruddles County and Best, Carlsberg. Food: There is a wide range of bar snacks ranging from homemade soup, roll and butter (£1), through chicken kiev (£3.75) to sirloin steak and chips (£6.50). Sandwiches start at £1.10 and there is an exceptionally good value three course Sunday lunch (£4.95) for which you must book. Telephone: (07515) 247.

Leaving the pub, turn left and follow the
road towards Cropton and Pickering.
After a short distance, turn right down a
cul-de-sac marked 'No Through Road'. When the
metalled road ends, a clearly defined path lies ahead.
This climbs steeply until you reach a wooden gate
leading onto a road, at which point you fork left
through the hamlet of Spaunton. At the T-junction
at the end of the village street, turn left (No Through
Road). Almost immediately, you pass through a gate
which gives access to a broad and well-defined track
through undulating fields. When you reach a junction
of footpaths with three bridleway signs, follow the
right-hand path through two gates, keeping the line of
trees on your right. In the right-hand corner of the
field, pass through a further gate which leads into
Spring Wood. The path skirts the edge of the wood
and then turns sharply left. As soon as you emerge
from the wood, ignore the stile on your left, and keep
on the tree-lined path. At a T-junction with the track
to Lingmoor Farm, turn right. Keep straight on,
passing a track to your left, following the track down
to the river and main road at the southern end of
Hutton le Hole village. Turn right up the village
street back to the car park.

St Mary's Church, Lastingham
In AD654, Cedd, a monk from
Lindisfarne, began to build
monastery here, and after his
death, his brother Chad
completed it. Unfortunately, the
building was destroyed in
AD866 and lay in ruins until
1078 when Stephen, Abbot of
Whitby began to restore it by
building a crypt as a shrine to St
Cedd. Stephen moved to York in
1086, so the monastery was
never completed. However, the
crypt, with chancel, nave and
two aisles, is a complete church
within the church, and now is
used for special services.

Kettlewell *to* Starbotton

Approximately 5 miles

River and hillside crag walk with good views up onto the crags and across lush meadowland. Along the riverbank path, look out for birds such as the dipper, grey wagtail, the occasional buzzard soaring, or herons and even kingfishers in the more sheltered waters.

Parking

OS Map 98 Ref SD9672
Kettlewell car park

Further exploration

Kettlewell

This is a typical dale village, with stone buildings following the streams up valley. Once a thriving community revitalised by lead-mining – the remains of the smelting mill can be seen on the confluence of streams 1\2 mile above the village – Kettlewell today is a popular tourist centre.

*T*urn right out of the car park and cross the River Wharfe over New Bridge. On the far side, bear right and take the lower gate on the footpath which follows the river. The path is the Dales Way – a long distance route linking Ilkley to Windermere. Follow the waymarked route, soon reaching a footbridge where four routes converge. Bear right over the bridge and follow the track up to a road. Turn left into Starbotton, with its huddled group of stone houses and farms. The pub lies at far end of village.

Fox and Hounds (Free House)

Beautifully situated in the heart of the valley, this white-painted pub is snug and welcoming, with a large stone fireplace in the small bar. Beamed ceilings with old copper lamps hanging, an antique settle and other solid old-fashioned furniture, add to the welcoming atmosphere. An inner room has wheelback chairs, flagstone floor, bric-a-brac and cooking pots dotted around. Outside seating is provided by sturdy tables and benches in a sheltered corner in front of the inn, with fine views of the hillsides over the roofs of this quiet hamlet.

On draught: Theakston Best and Old Peculiar, Younger's Scotch, Guinness, Carlsberg, Bourne Original cider. Food: Good standard bar food includes soup (£1.20), sandwiches (from £1.30), ploughmans (from £2.25), and pizza (£3.50). Food is served at 12-2pm (evenings in the summer only). Closed Thursday lunch, and all day Monday Nov-May. Telephone: (075676) 269.

*R*etrace your steps to the footbridge and follow the path waymarked to Arncliffe, climbing left up the south-west side of the valley. The early part of this route up the hillside follows along a narrow, walled lane which was once part of an ancient packhorse trail, a trade route between dales. When the lane becomes a path through a gate, continue climbing across pasture to a wall running along the length of the fellside. Cross the ladder stile over the wall, and bear left towards Moor End Farm, keeping the wall to your left. Cross a stile, follow the path through a gateway and continue on the waymarked route around the farmhouse. Leave the farm through the gate ahead and follow bridleway back to Kettlewell and the car park.

Hadrian's Wall *to* Haltwhistle

Approximately 7 miles.

This is a strenuous, but very enjoyable walk, with many variations of scenery, from the wall itself to the trail through the woods by the stream, and finally the open countryside leading to the Peat Steel Crags – a bonus when you least expect it. Look for the kingfishers and dippers as you walk along the banks of the river.

Parking
OS Map 87 Ref NY7166
Walltown car park.

Further Exploration
Roman Army Museum
Standing next to Walltown Crags, one of the highest wall sections, this museum has been designed to introduce the history of Carvoran (the Roman fort of Magna) and Hadrian's Wall. Telephone: (06972) 485.

Climb to the remains of the watchtower on the wall and take the trail to the right, following the line of the old wall, past another watch tower. Cross several stone walls by the ladder stiles until you reach a small coppice. Follow the footpath through the copse to reach another stile. Cross this stile, pass a farm cottage on your left, and cross two more stiles and fields towards some farm buildings. With the farm buildings on your left, head for the stone wall ahead and cross the stile, and three more stiles and fields to finally reach another stile adjacent to a bridge over a stream. Cross the road into Cowfield picnic area. With the stream on your left, continue on the track to a sign indicating the Roman Wall. Turn right here through a kissing gate, and follow the track across the field to the road, and you will soon reach the pub.

Milecastle Inn (Free House)

This comfortable and attractive pub is particularly celebrated for its food. The bar is popular and cosy, furnished with dark wood tables and tapestry-style upholstery, and there is a welcoming log fire in cooler months. While walkers are welcome, their muddy boots and dogs are not.

On draught: Webster Yorkshire, Ruddles Best and County, Guinness, Fosters, Carlsberg, Strongbow cider. Food: A wide-ranging menu includes soup (95p), steak (£6.50), chicken kiev (£4.25), seafood platter (£4.35), vegetarian spring rolls (£3), ploughmans (£2.70), and sandwiches (£1.50). Food is served at 12-2pm and 6.30-9pm. Booking is essential in the restaurant area. Telephone: (0434) 320682.

*T*ake the road to the left of the pub, uphill until you reach a sign to Haltwhistle Burn on your right. Follow this track down to pass some cottages on your right. Immediately after these cottages, follow the footpath off to the right, away from the track and descend towards the river, passing a disused chimney, to reach a track which leads down towards a kissing gate and a bridge. Cross the bridge and follow the track, keeping the stream on your left. The track finally reaches a road into which you turn left. Just before a white cottage, cross a stone stile on your right, and strike diagonally across the paddock to the right where there is an iron gate. Through the gate, climb the wooded bank to reach an open field, head towards the farm buildings and pass through the farmyard gates to reach the road. Turn right here and continue up the hill to reach the B6318. Cross the road and stile, following the route to Lowtown. This climbs over the hill and passes through a gate in the wall ahead. From here, strike diagonally left to reach the Peat Steel Crags. Descend and cross to a gate with a blue route marker. Pass through and continue straight, crossing the remains of two stone walls to reach another gate with a blue marker, with a derelict cottage to your left. Turn left and follow the Vellam Road over three cattle grids to return to the car park.

Baybridge *to* Blanchland   Approximately 5 miles

A pleasant walk through farmland and along the Derwent river. Watch out for pied and grey wagtails and curlews.

Parking
OS Map 87 Ref NY9549
Baybridge car park and picnic area

*L*eave the picnic area and cross the road to find a track along the left bank of the river, signposted to Blanchland. Continue on this path, crossing several stiles on the way, to Blanchland, where the path leads to the left of the bridge, across the road and immediately right behind the wall of the bridge to reach the river bank again. Follow the river past three buildings on your left, the last being a derelict barn. Here the path becomes a track which you follow between two stone walls away from the river. At the top, this bears round to the left to reach a metalled road. Follow the road to the left back to Blanchland, turn left and the pub is on your left.

Lord Crewe Arms (Free House)

Originally an abbot's dwelling for the nearby abbey, part of the cloisters can still be seen in the inn's terraced gardens. There are huge fireplaces in the bars, with one of the 13th-century inglenooks containing a priest hole. One of the bars is down in a crypt which has a stone-flagged arched roof, and is furnished with pews. The main bar has fine beams, old settles, and numerous photographs adorn the walls. The inn is named after an eighteenth-century aristocrat Lord Crewe, Bishop of Durham who owned the village and on his death, left it to a trust to ensure it remained unaltered. Children are welcome in the restaurant.

On draught: Vaux Samson, Walkers Lorimers Scotch, Carlsberg, McEwan, Guinness. Food: The menu includes soup (£1.30), filled granary rolls (£1.75 £2.25), grilled pork and apple burgers with chips and salad (£3.95), and fillet of cod with peas, mushrooms and chips (£4). Food is served at 12-2pm and 7-9pm (9.30 at weekends). Telephone: (0434) 675251.

Turn right out of the pub and take the second track on your right just before you reach the car park. Bear left between two stone walls and follow the track up into the woods, keeping the stone shed on your right. The path meets a grass track which you follow to the left until you reach an iron gate. Through this gate, turn left across the field to reach another gate leading to a metalled road, with cottages on your right. Turn right along the road until you see a gate and a track on the right which leads back from the road. Follow the track through the gate to an iron gate in a stone wall. Pass through the gate and strike diagonally left to climb onto Penny Pie Fell, bearing northwest. As you reach the top, you will see a black barn on the fell ahead of you. Keep the wall on your left and cross a small stream to pass on the left-hand side of the barn. The track continues straight through an iron gate in a stone wall, then through another immediately on your right. From here, head diagonally left over the crest of the hill to reach another iron gate in a wall, and another at the lower right-hand corner. The track descends to the left to reach Penny Pie House, and your route follows it away to the right of the farm after crossing a stream. With the wall on your left, continue along the track which eventually becomes a metalled road, passing through a wooded area. There are two more iron gates to pass through before finally reaching the road at Baybridge. Turn right here and return to the picnic area.

Further Exploration

Blanchland

This small, isolated village is thought to be named after the white habits of the Premonstratensian monks who settled there in the 12th century. The present church was built in 1752 using those parts of the old abbey church which had survived. There are three fine medieval tombstones on the transept floor, and many interesting artefacts.

Threlkeld *to* Scales

Approximately 5 miles

A low level walk along pretty river banks and the edges of the fells, with good views of northern Lakeland peaks.

Parking

OS Ref NY318256 Threlkeld car park just north of the village on Blease road to Blencathra.

Further Exploration

St. Mary's Church, Threlkeld
While the present church dates from the 18th century, the original church is 14th century and may be the oldest chapelry in the Diocese of Carlisle.

*L*eave the car park on a public footpath to Threlkeld through a kissing gate. The path follows Blease Gill down to the village. At the road, turn right, and then left onto a public footpath along the side of St Mary's church. Cross a stile into a field which you then leave by a stile near the opposite corner. Cross the A66 and turn left to find another stile into a field on the right. Follow the path along the edge of the field, cross a stile by the River Glenderamackin and turn left to follow the path along the river bank. Cross a narrow footbridge over a small stream and continue along the main river bank. Cross over a minor road and follow the signpost to Guardhouse. The path continues for about a mile, crossing a metalled track to Keswick golf course, and a small stream. When the path turns left away from the river alongside a stream, cross a footbridge to reach a metalled track. Turn right and, just before Guardhouse bridge, you will see two public footpaths on your left. Take the path to Stone Raise which follows the river bank, then bears left along a fence. Continue to follow the fence as it bends sharply left, and cross the stile at the corner of the field. Bear right across the next field to pass to the left of a line of oak trees, heading in the direction of a whitewashed house. Leave this field by the stile ahead and the next field by a stile in the top right-hand corner. Follow the right edge of the next field to reach the A66. Turn right along the road and you will soon see the pub.

White Horse Inn (Free House)

 This whitewashed pub set into the hillside has no garden and only a single bench for eating outside. However, there is plenty of seating in the smart, spacious oak-beamed bar which also has an open fire and is decorated with pictures of hunting scenes and trophies. Children under 5 are not allowed inside.

On draught: Jennings Bitter and Mild, Guinness, Hansa. There is also a range of malt whiskies. Food: A home-cooked lunchtime menu includes peach halves with garlic cream cheese pate and wholemeal bread, hot savoury flan of the day (both £2.95), ploughmans (£3.25) and Cumberland sausage with salad (£4.75). Sweets include sticky toffee ginger pudding (£1.95) and fudge ice cream (£1.75). A more extensive menu is available in the evening, but it is advisable to book. Food is served at 12-1.30pm and 7-8.30pm (not Monday or Tuesday evenings). Telephone: (07687) 79241.

*T*urn right out of the pub and walk along the main road to reach a small house. Turn right up a farm track, go through a kissing gate in the stone wall ahead, and turn left onto the fells. Continue to follow the path along the fellfoot, keeping the stone wall on your left. You will cross Scales Beck, pass Doddick Farm and then cross Doddick Gill. The path crosses a third stream (Gate Gill) and then continues through a gate in the same direction along the fellfoot. After crossing two stiles, pass through a gate in front of Blease Gill and turn left before the stream to go through a second gate. Follow the path signposted to Threlkeld down the stream to reach the car park.

Crosthwaite *to* Strawberry Bank

Approximately 7 miles.

A fairly level walk through pastoral agricultural scenes and lush ferned woodland at Cartmel Fell.

Parking
OS Map 97 Ref SD4491.
Crosthwaite church

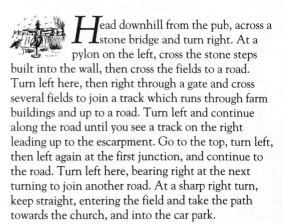

*F*rom the car park, turn left and walk through the village, turning right at Starnthwaite to reach a signposted stile on the left. Over the stile, bear left, then right after the next stile. Join a paved lane and follow the arrows to a ladder stile, after which you walk down the left side of the field, turning left again at the corner. Walk on the right side of the next few fields, turning right at a bridleway, and left at a road. Turn right at the next junction and follow the next footpath on the left to Lamb Howe. At a house, turn left, following arrows into the woods, and then bear right at a fork. Reaching a road, turn right, then left at the bridleway. At an old barn, turn left then, at a road, turn right and left again onto another bridleway. Continue straight through the gates and on to Hollins Farm, up to the road, and the pub is on the right.

*H*ead downhill from the pub, across a stone bridge and turn right. At a pylon on the left, cross the stone steps built into the wall, then cross the fields to a road. Turn left here, then right through a gate and cross several fields to join a track which runs through farm buildings and up to a road. Turn left and continue along the road until you see a track on the right leading up to the escarpment. Go to the top, turn left, then left again at the first junction, and continue to the road. Turn left here, bearing right at the next turning to join another road. At a sharp right turn, keep straight, entering the field and take the path towards the church, and into the car park.

Masons Arms (Free House)

 This is a lovely remote, whitewashed pub with a large kitchen range, ancient country furniture and a tiny but astonishingly stocked bar. Children are welcome until 9pm.

On draught: 200 brands feature on the beer list, from Chinese Tsingtao to Venezuelan Polar Beer, along with solid British ales such as Thwaites, Younger's No 3, and two homebrews. Food: An adventurous menu includes stuffed vine leaves (£3.25) and Cajun chicken (£4.95). Food is served at 12-2pm and 6-8.45pm. Telephone: (04488) 486.

Grasmere *to* Elterwater

Approximately 6 miles

Follow in William Wordsworth's footsteps on this beautiful walk through the more accessible Lakeland fells. Fairly steep climbing in places requires some effort but the spectacular views will make it worthwhile.

Parking

OS Map 90 NY3307 There are a number of car parks in Grasmere.

Further Exploration

St Oswald's Church, Grasmere
The impressive interior of this church is thought to be unique, and has been described by Wordsworth in the Vth Book of the *Excursion*. The poet's prayer book is featured among other interesting items in the show-case behind the stalls, and the grave he shares with his wife Mary, lies beneath one of the eight yew trees he planted in the churchyard. The graves of his sister and her two children, are also nearby, as are those of Hartley Coleridge, Anne Clough, the Rev. Joseph Sympson (*Excursion* vii.,ll 31-291), the Lake artist William Green, and Sir John Richardson, the distinguished Arctic explorer.

*F*rom the front of the parish church, turn left over the bridge and follow the road to the A591. Take the road opposite, past Dove Cottage, and continue for about a mile back to the A591. Turn left, then take a footpath to the right at White Moss Common. At the River Rothay, turn right, cross the footbridge and take the path straight ahead, signposted to Rydal Woods and Loughrigg Terrace. At the end of the woods, through a kissing gate, turn right along a path signposted to High Close and Langdale, to the top of the ridge. Turn left along Loughrigg Terrace, straight on through a kissing gate and follow the main path to a road. Turn right, soon to take a clearly marked public footpath off to the left. Pass through a kissing gate, descend through a wood, go through another kissing gate and turn left and left again, passing through a gate. Climb along the edge of the wood, keeping a stone wall on your left, through a gate to the top. Continue on the path down to the village, keeping slightly left, cross the minor road and follow the path down to the B5343. Cross the road, turn left and, very shortly, take the minor road on the right into Elterwater. The pub is at the crossroads in the middle of the village.

Britannia Inn (Free House)

This pretty whitewashed pub overlooking the village green, is more than 400 years old. Popular with locals and walkers alike, the beamed main bar and slate-floored snug can get quite crowded at times. There is plenty of room outside to enjoy a welcome rest and refreshments.

On draught: Harlteys XB, Marston Pedigree, Jennings Mild and Premium, Guinness, Carling Black Label, Tennents Extra, and Bulmer's Traditional cider. There is also a small selection of country wines and a wide range of malt whiskies. Food: A wide selection of excellent home-cooked food includes chicken and broccoli bake, pork chops with cider, Cumberland sausage, and cheese and onion quiche (all around £4). Delicious sweets (£1.60) include butterscotch and walnut fudge cake and raspberry meringue gateau. Food is served at 12-2pm and 6.30-9pm. There is a separate restaurant (evenings only) providing set four-course meals at around £13. Telephone: (09667) 210.

Turn right out of the pub, cross the bridge and immediately turn right up the road running alongside Great Langdale Beck. Just before the slate quarry, turn right on the marked footpath down to the river, then cross the river to reach the road. Turn right and, after a short distance, take the footpath on the left through two kissing gates, along and across a small stream, and to the right of a field to reach a minor road. Turn right, then left up a footpath towards Spedding Crag. Opposite the slate quarry, turn left up the main path, ignoring the minor path that goes straight on, and continue to climb very steeply. At the top, cross a path and keep straight on along, and then across, a small stream, to reach a stone wall. Turn left and continue, with the wall on your right, crossing a number of small streams. At the junction with another path by a cairn, turn right, still following the wall. Through a kissing gate, continue downhill, through more gates to a road. Turn left to a junction, then turn right, following the Ambleside sign to return to the church.

Dove Cottage, Grasmere
Wordsworth's home from 1799 to 1808, Dove Cottage was where he wrote *Michael, Resolution and Independence, Ode: Imitations of Immorality,* and completed *The Prelude.* Visitors are offered guided tours of the cottage, and are free to explore the garden.

Wordsworth Museum, Grasmere
The poet's life and work are illustrated with manuscripts, portraits and memorabilia in this museum adjacent to the cottage. Telephone: (09665) 544 and 547.

Aira Force *to* Dockray

Approximately 5 miles

A fine walk with waterfalls, open fells and magnificent views of Ullswater.

Parking
OS Map 96 & 97 Ref NY4020
Aira Force car park.

*F*ollow the footpath across Aira Beck and when you reach a fork, bear left, following the path upstream to the waterfall. Continue through a wicket fence into the woods, then past the Higher Falls. Another wicket gate in a wall leads to open fields, and then you follow the sign for Dockray. You will emerge onto a paved road through farm buildings, and the pub is directly ahead.

Royal (Whitbread)

This is a lovely old, whitewashed pub well in keeping with its Lakeland setting, having originally been a 16th-century coaching inn. Copper is a feature throughout the bars – coal buckets, toasting forks, warming pans – and walls are decorated with prints of various styles. Next to the large garden is a field which is the home of geese, chickens, and a famous goat called Louie. Children are welcome.

On draught: Castle Eden, Pedigree, Trophy, Guinness, Heineken, Stella Artois, Bulmer's Original cider. There is also a good selection of wines by the glass or bottle. Food: Lunches include potted shrimps with salad and a roll (£2.25), homemade steak pie and chips (£4.25), soup and a roll (£1), and salads (£4.25). Puddings include hot chocolate fudge cake with mint choc chip ice-cream and sticky toffee pudding with cream (both £1.60). The evening menu is more extensive. Food is served at 12-2pm and 6-9pm (only Friday - Sunday out of season, all week in season) and morning coffee is also available. Telephone: (07684) 82356

*T*urn right out of the pub, then right again beside a green shed, through a gate onto Watermillock Common. Bear left, proceeding across the common. In the distance are two hillocks and a depression to their right. Aim for the higher ground to the right of this depression, crossing some usually soggy grassland, until you reach a stone wall. Turn right and walk along the wall for about a mile. When you reach three scree slopes on your right, go through the opening in the wall just past the last slope, and turn left to follow the steep grassy path downhill, across a stile and on until you reach a road. Go through the car park opposite, turn right and head down towards your car park.

Further Exploration

Dalemain

This stately home was originally a medieval peel tower, extended in the Tudor era and then completed in 1745, and the furnishings reflect the different styles of these periods. The tower contains a yeomanry museum, and there is also a countryside museum in the 16th-century cobbled courtyard. The grounds include a deer park, extensive gardens – famous for rare trees and shrubs – and an adventure playground. Telephone: (07684) 86450.

Belle Grange *to* Near Sawrey

Approximately 6½ miles

A pleasant walk through National Trust forest and across Claife Heights into Beatrix Potter country, with spectacular views of Windermere from the lake's quiet side.

Parking

OS Map 97 Ref SD3899. Follow signs for the ferry to reach the car park.

Further Exploration

Hill Top, Near Sawrey (National Trust)

The house where Beatrix Potter wrote many of her books, is directly behind the Tower Bank Arms. This little 17th-century house contains the writer's furniture and china, and her 'New Room' where she did much of her work, was restored in 1986. Telephone: (09666) 269.

Not far from Belle Grange is Hawkshead Grammer School where William Wordsworth went to school. It is open daily from March to October.

*F*ollow the path to Belle Grange House, and at the first house on your right, bear right and continue straight on through the forest, eventually following the signs for Sawrey. Pass between the two halves of Wise Een Tarn, on to Moss Eccles Tarn and into Near Sawrey. Bear left for the pub.

Tower Bank Arms (Free House)

This small 17th-century country inn made an appearance in Beatrix Potter's tale of Jemima Puddleduck, and is now owned by the National Trust. The interior is traditional and simply furnished with settles on the slate floor, and a big wood-burning stove. There is a pleasant garden, and children are allowed in the eating area.

On draught: Theakston XB and Old Peculiar, Matthew Brown Lion Mild, Beck's, Strongbow cider. There is a thoughtful selection of reasonably priced wines, and even champagne. Food: Home-cooked meals include chicken breast filled with stilton and leeks (£6), cream cheese and broccoli pie (£3.50) and, of course, sticky toffee pudding. Food is served at 12-2pm and 6.30-9pm (till 7pm on Sundays). Telephone: (09666) 334.

*R*etrace your steps uphill to the turning for Far Sawrey. Follow the path to a metalled road, turn left and, immediately after the pub, left again up the track signposted to Claife Heights. At the next fork, bear right and pass through a gate. Follow the main path which will eventually take you through the woods and to the lake. Follow the lakeside path back to the car park.